"Packed with essential, honest, practical information for the alcoholic and her family, *Women and Recovery* draws on Dr. Harris' professional expertise, wise advice, and personal story to show the reader how to find a fulfilling new life."

—Paula D'Arcy, author of *Waking up to This Day*

"For years, there has been an alarming lack of resources specifically for women with alcohol problems. This book fills that void by intelligently combining forthright personal accounts of alcoholism with treatment and recovery science. The result is a compelling, engaging, and, above all, useful book that will open the door to a better life for countless women."

—John F. Kelly, Ph.D., Associate Professor in Psychiatry,
Harvard Medical School; Director Addiction Recovery
Management Service, Massachusetts General Hospital

"Where was this book when my mother needed it? *Women and Recovery: Finding Hope* is a wonderful and very comforting resource for women and family members. I really enjoyed it."

—Susan Ford Bales, daughter of Betty Ford

"*Women and Recovery* is a must read. Dr. Harris gets it—one size fits all has never fit women. Her page-turning vignettes about binge-drinking girls, social-drinking moms, and others illustrate the many ways women slip into alcoholism. With her unique coping skills, Dr. Harris offers a lifesaving ring of hope to women and their loved ones."

—Karen Tandy, former Administrator,
U.S. Drug Enforcement Administration

"Kitty Harris knows that women who drink too much will resist the strategies that lead to breaking the cycle of addiction unless they trust the messenger. By telling her own story of recovery using straight, blunt, and sober talk, Kitty supports women in recovery who choose to live their second chance in a qualitatively different life. It is this combination of hope and a solution specifically directed at women that gives *Women in Recovery* a vital and prominent position in the recovery literature."

—Dorie Evensen, Ph.D., Professor of Education, Penn State University

Women and Recovery

Finding Hope

KITTY S. HARRIS, Ph.D.,
WITH JODIE GOULD

WILEY
John Wiley & Sons, Inc.

Design by Forty-Five Degree Design, LLC

Published by John Wiley & Sons, Inc., Hoboken, New Jersey
Published simultaneously in Canada

For general information about our other products and services, please contact our Customer Care Department within the United States at (800) 762-2974, outside the United States at (317) 572-3993 or fax (317) 572-4002.

Wiley also publishes its books in a variety of electronic formats and by print-on-demand. Some content that appears in standard print versions of this book may not be available in other formats. For more information about Wiley products, visit us at www.wiley.com.

Library of Congress Cataloging-in-Publication Data

Harris, Kitty S.
    Women and recovery: finding hope/Kitty S. Harris with Jodie Gould.
        p. cm.
    Includes bibliographical references and index.
    ISBN 978-0-470-94183-6 (pbk.); ISBN 978-1-118-21733-7 (ebk);
    ISBN 978-1-118-21734-4 (ebk); ISBN 978-1-118-21735-1 (ebk)
1. Women alcoholics—Rehabilitation.   I. Gould, Jodie.   II. Title.
HV5137.H37 2012
616.86'10082—dc23

                                                        2011046740

Printed in the United States of America

10 9 8 7 6 5 4 3 2 1

This book is dedicated to all the courageous women who walked before me on the road we call recovery—most especially: Betty, Irene, and Pitsy.

To Sylva, D'Ann and Shyrle, and to all of the loving women who walked beside me.

Finally, to Mandy, Leigh, and Peyton and to all of the resilient women who will walk down this road after me.

To all of these brave women, I paraphrase the words of St. Francis of Assisi: "Start by doing what's necessary, then do what's possible. Suddenly you will find that you are doing the impossible."

—Kitty Harris

To my beloved daughter, Samantha, who at age ten, is developing the kind of self-confidence and independent thinking that will help her make good decisions during what will surely be some challenging years ahead.

To my husband, Robert Katel, for his unflagging support; my mother, for her maternal wisdom; my sister, whose advice I depend on; and to my brother-in-law Rick Tieszen, for his brilliance and positive spirit.

—Jodie Gould

Contents

Part Two
BREAKING THE CYCLE OF ADDICTION

Acknowledgments

It is a well-known truth in my field that no one really succeeds on his or her own—we all have the blessings of others who help us along the way. This book is an example of that principle. I would like to thank Jodie Gould, who made the initial contact that started this project. She has been a joy to work with and gave voice not only to the pain of addiction but also to the hope of recovery. My agent, Linda Konner, took a total novice and walked me through the publishing maze with patience and understanding. I would like to express appreciation to our editors, Tom Miller and Jorge Amaral, whose guidance and support directed us to a well-defined finished product. In addition to our editors, thanks go to Christel Winkler, Kimberly Monroe-Hill, and the other individuals throughout John Wiley & Sons for their support. I am grateful to my assistant, Ann Casiraghi, who was always willing to help with research and references that needed to be verified, and to Dr. Beth Robinson who, as a graduate student, engaged in hours of brainstorming for the genesis of the recovery model. I have tremendous gratitude for all of the women who agreed to be interviewed for this book. Their honesty and courage inspire me. Additionally, I acknowledge that this book is a reflection of thirty-two years of participating in recovery meetings, reading hundreds of books and journals on addiction and recovery, and attending seminars, conferences, and workshops that address the issues of addictive disorders. Thank you to all who have shaped my ideas, concepts, and vision of the pain of addiction and the hope of recovery.

My friends through the years have had such a significant effect on my life. These friendships have always been one of the most treasured aspects in my life. Bless you for all of the time, energy, and love that you have invested in me—I would not be the person who I am today without your handprint on my heart.

Finally, I would like to express my appreciation and love for my family, the people in my life who have mattered the most. Mom and Dad never waver in their love and support. My sister, Linn, stands by my side through the ups and downs and has always been there for me, as has my brother-in-law, David. My deep gratitude and love to my precious husband, Morris, who is a reflection of serenity and models for me the genuine meaning of living an authentic life. I am blessed!

—Kitty Harris

Thanks to Kitty Harris for being such a delightful coauthor. Every book I write, I learn something new, and Kitty showed me how pain knocks on everyone's door like an unwelcome guest. To Linda Konner, my agent and dear friend, who remains an integral part of my life and career. To our editors, Tom Miller and Jorge Amaral, whose expertise helped mold our book, and to the entire Wiley team for publishing this book for the women who need it most.

—Jodie Gould

Introduction

Women alcoholics are not a monolithic, one-size-fits-all group. The type of drinker you are depends on your age, your stage of life, and the pain that motivates your compulsive (the psychological term for "obsessive") behavior. If you are wondering whether you or someone you know is an alcoholic, there are quizzes in this book that will point out some of the red flags. Yet keep in mind that it's not only how *much* you drink or even the frequency but *how* you drink that determines whether you have an addiction.

The female alcoholics described in this book—from binge drinkers to closet drinkers—demonstrate several new and disturbing drinking trends among women. Some women drink when they are out with friends. Others drink only when they are alone. Some sneak sips during the day to stay high, while others wait impatiently until the clock strikes 5 p.m. before they start drinking.

One thing we know for sure about alcoholism is that it can strike anyone at any age (certain people start while still in primary school), and the type of drinker you are often depends on the stage of life you are in. As we move from one stage of life into another, be it from childhood to teen, teen to young adult, young adult to midlife, or middle age to senior, alcohol can seem to help ease our anxiety should the transition be a difficult one. If you're reading this book, chances are that either you drink or you know someone who does. Maybe you're a twenty-something who frequents bars at happy hour with your girlfriends, followed by some clubbing. Or perhaps you're a stay-at-home mom who finds cocktails as ubiquitous as juice boxes at your kids' playdates. You could also be a mother of a teen or a college-age girl who worries that your daughter's drinking is out of control.

Whatever the case may be, you are not alone. There are an estimated 15 million American alcoholics, a third of whom are women. Here are some other scary statistics: Approximately 5.3 million American women are currently drinking in a way that threatens their health or safety, according to the National Institute of Alcoholism Abuse and Addiction (NIAAA). Equally disturbing was a recent survey conducted by the Centers for Disease Control, which revealed that 6.7 million women, the majority between the ages of eighteen and twenty-four, engage in binge drinking (more than five drinks in one day).

During my thirty years as a counselor and an educator, I developed what I call the Core Recovery Process (CRP), which I will share with you in this book. It is a new model that helps people understand the process and the cycle of alcoholism and addiction. Equally important, it is a recovery paradigm that works and can be used with any twelve-step or other recovery program.

It's based on a simple premise. We all experience pain at some point in our lives, regardless of age, race, creed, or economic status. When people choose alcohol (or other chemicals or compulsive behaviors) to cope with the pain, they begin to feel normal again. What follows, however, is an avalanche of negative consequences that causes them to feel guilt, shame, and then more pain.

There are five basic areas of pain that people experience: physical (injury, disease, or violence), mental (depression or anxiety), emotional (hurt, rejection, disappointment, anger, or fear), social (isolation and feelings that you don't belong), and spiritual (loss of faith, hope, and purpose in life). The pain doesn't have to be enormous, but it is almost always chronic, which means it never goes away on its own—thus the desire to self-medicate.

If we continue to self-medicate to ease our pain and in an attempt to feel normal again, we will eventually experience negative consequences. We often alienate people we love, such as our families and friends, and we take risks with our lives and others', sometimes even our own children's, by getting behind the wheel of a car while drinking or drunk. We might get in trouble with our families, at work, at school, financially, or with the law. When this happens, we inevitably feel guilt and shame. We start to hate ourselves for hurting the people we cherish most. Guilt can be a good thing when it stops us from diving further into the abyss, but shame and self-loathing can also cause us to cycle back to the pain, which prompts us to drink even more.

This is why the traditional form of intervention doesn't always work. When a friend or a family member says, "If you really loved me, you would stop," the guilt and pain we feel only exacerbates the problem. I'm not suggesting that families and friends shouldn't intervene or that alcoholics shouldn't make amends to those whom they have hurt (they should), but I've found that in order to give alcoholics the help they need, building up their self-esteem works much better than tearing it down. We do this by teaching alcoholics healthy coping skills. Once positive events on the path to recovery occur in an alcoholic's life, a remarkable transition takes place: she begins to develop resiliency. Resiliency is the ability to bounce back after being knocked down. Recovery is not only about being sober; it's about learning the skills that make you more resilient.

Women and Recovery will teach you new ways to deal with your pain or to help others who are suffering. It also explores the latest drinking trends among girls and women of all ages—from those who binge drink in order to get the quickest high and momtini mothers, whose boozy children's birthday parties and playdates help them cope with the monotony of motherhood, to closet drinkers who sip their white wine (or harder stuff) in the privacy of their own pantries. As thirty-three-year-old Jennifer R. explained in her stayathomemotherdom blog: [I am a] "mom to 4-year-old Ian and 1-year-old Isabel in recovery from alcoholism and attempting to find serenity in a life filled with temper tantrums, dirty diapers and Power Rangers."

The type of pain that women experience varies with each individual. It might stem from abusive partners, child-care issues, social anxiety, or a poor body image, all of which drive many women to drink. Adolescent girls and young women are particularly susceptible to the way alcohol is marketed, which makes it even more difficult to resist. I'm not suggesting that everyone should give up alcohol—there's nothing wrong with enjoying a glass of wine or a cocktail every now and then or even daily, if you are not an alcoholic. If you are an alcoholic, though, you must find healthy alternatives to cope with your pain. When I am feeling down, for example, I run. Thirty-two years ago, I ran to a wine bottle.

Of course, there are many more types of female alcoholics than the ones described in this book, and some women straddle several categories. It doesn't matter, however, what category of drinker you or your loved one fall into. Remember that you can stop if you are willing to accept the help you need. It might take a while, and you may have to hit bottom first, but no one has to go through life drunk and miserable. If you recognize yourself or someone you love in these scenarios, please read the resources section at the end of the book for information on whom to call and where to go for assistance. Whatever you do, don't do it alone. There are so many resources available to help people recover from addiction. With determination and effort, you can become one of the millions of success stories.

Part One

WOMEN WHO DRINK TOO MUCH

Quiz: Alcohol IQ*

Think you know a lot about alcohol and drinking? Take this "bar exam" on health, designated driving, fetal alcohol syndrome, drunk driving, and other alcohol-related topics. See the answers below the quiz to analyze your alcohol IQ.

Read each question and answer true or false.

1. Compared to a bottle of beer, a glass of white wine is a good choice for someone who wants a light drink with less alcohol.
2. Drinking black coffee is a good way to "sober up."
3. The Puritans loaded more beer than water onto the *Mayflower* before they sailed for the New World.
4. The Women's Christian Temperance Union still exists.
5. Switching among beer, wine, and spirits will lead to intoxication more quickly than sticking to one form of alcohol beverage.
6. High-protein foods such as peanuts and cheese slow the absorption of alcohol into the body.
7. The more educated people are in the United States, the more likely they are to drink alcoholic beverages.
8. Although smaller, a glass of wine contains more alcohol than a can of beer.

---

* This quiz was excerpted from a post created by David J. Hanson, Ph.D., of the State University of New York at Potsdam, www.alcohol.bitglyph.com (2007).

9. Distillation was developed during the Middle Ages.
10. It's okay to drive when you've been drinking, if you believe you are sober.

Answers

1. **False.** A typical glass of red or white wine, a bottle of beer, or a drink of spirits (rum, whiskey, tequila, and so on) each contains an almost identical amount of pure alcohol.
2. **False.** Unfortunately, only time will help a drunk person get sober. On average, the body needs about one hour to "burn off" any typical drink. Alcohol typically stays in your system for ten hours.
3. **True.** The Puritans, including their children, enjoyed beer, wine, and liquor in moderation. It was the rare Puritan who did not imbibe some form of alcohol.
4. **True.** The Women's Christian Temperance Union, which was formed during the Prohibition Era, is currently a nationwide organization of twenty-five thousand members and actively attempts to influence public policy concerning alcohol. For example, it is currently active in efforts to ban all ads for alcoholic beverages from TV.
5. **False.** The level of blood alcohol content is what determines sobriety or intoxication. Remember that standard drinks of beer, wine, and spirits contain equivalent amounts of alcohol.
6. **True.** Eating, especially high-protein foods, and carefully pacing the consumption of drinks can help prevent or delay intoxication.
7. **True.** The more educated people are, the more likely they are to drink.
8. **False.** The typical bottle of beer, glass of wine, and drink of spirits has about the same amount of alcohol. To a breathalyzer, they are the same.
9. **True.** The resulting alcohol was called aqua vitae, or "water of life."
10. **False.** Protect others and yourself by never driving when you've been drinking, regardless of how you may feel. It's always best to use a designated driver.

1

My Story

There are numerous drinking memoirs in the canon of alcohol-related literature. Caroline Knapp's *Drinking: A Love Story*, *Wishful Drinking* by Carrie Fisher, and *Smashed: The Story of a Drunken Girlhood* by Doren Zailckas are a few notable examples, all of which chronicle the disintegration and subsequent rehabilitation of otherwise smart, talented women due to alcoholism. They are cautionary tales well worth reading, but this book is not about *my* drinking experiences. It is about other women who, like me, got lost in their addiction and, more important, how anyone who wants to can climb her way out of the alcoholic abyss. Yet I will share a bit about my journey as a recovering alcoholic who has subsequently devoted her life to helping others find peace and happiness through sobriety. Many people who are unfamiliar with this disease believe, as I once did, that alcoholics are not upstanding members of society. They imagine drunks as sweat-soaked hobos who populate shelters, prisons, and the streets—grisly ghosts of their formerly sober selves. Yet as this book will attest, many women alcoholics do not live under a bridge but rather under the radar. They hide their secrets from the world like flasks tucked into their purses. Alcoholics look and act like you and me. Yes, I've included a number of despairing stories about women alcoholics that will bring tears to your eyes, but my experience as an alcoholic was not like a *Lifetime* movie. I was what is now known as a "functional alcoholic." I spent four years hiding my drinking problem from my family, friends, and colleagues. I did not break into a million little pieces, but I did fall apart like a tipsy Humpty Dumpty and put myself back together again. I was one of the thousands of ordinary woman whom you pass on the street, stand behind in the supermarket line, sit next to at your workplace, or organize with at PTA meetings. You wouldn't pick me out of a crowd and say, "She's an alcoholic." In fact, I didn't even know that I had a drinking problem. I simply thought I drank a bit too much and could stop at any time.

An Idyllic Childhood

Another misconception about alcoholics is that all of them are products of unhappy, abusive, or emotionally deprived childhoods. If that were true, why are there so many raging alcoholics among the middle and privileged classes? I had always been a devout Christian who was committed to the spiritual principles of faith, hope, and helping others, but as anyone familiar with addiction knows, alcoholism crosses every religion, race, ethnic, or class line. The reason someone becomes an addict is deceptively simple. We drink or take drugs to cope with our pain, and, as I mentioned earlier, human suffering is universal. My sister and I had an idyllic childhood surrounded by a loving, supportive, and financially secure family. Everything had always come easy to me, both socially and academically. My father, who worked as a salesman for a large corporation, was often promoted and transferred, so we moved around a lot while I was growing up. We lived in many cities, including Baltimore, Pittsburgh, Jacksonville, and Chicago. Despite our peripatetic lifestyle, I had lots of friends and a lot of love. When I was in high school, my dad decided that he had had enough of the corporate culture, and we moved to Texas, my mom's home state.

As a teenager I studied hard, participated in the debate team, and, unlike many of my peers, avoided alcohol and drugs. This wasn't because my parents didn't drink—they did. My dad always told me, "If you want to drink, just do it at home." Yet I was the classic geek who'd rather hang out at a library than at a bar.

After graduation, I went to college nearby and joined a sorority, whose members were also studious and serious girls like me, so I was able to continue abstaining from alcohol. Not that my sorority sisters didn't have the occasional party. When they did, I was always the designated driver. I met a guy on the debate team, and we dated all through college.

After college, I went immediately to graduate school, where I got a master's in communications. Wanting to continue my education even further, I applied for a doctoral program. In the meantime, I took a job as a teacher at a local high school. This is when my life took a downward turn. The principal at my school began to pressure me to do unethical things, such as change students' grades so they could stay on the football team. When I refused, he changed the grades behind my back. I was so young and naive, and I thought this was just the way things were in work world. I dreaded getting up in the morning and going to work, but I needed the money. Every day got increasingly worse as time went on. My boss, who was getting his master's degree, asked me to write his papers for him. As an innocent, churchgoing girl, I knew that what he was asking (actually, demanding) me to do was wrong. When I refused, he said, "You'll pay for that!"

And I did. This unscrupulous principal, who was married and twenty years my senior, started to sexually harass me by making inappropriate and flirtatious comments. He even showed up unannounced at my house one weekend. He tried to bribe me by saying, "If you do this for me, I will make things better for you here." I told a few of my friends what was going on (remember, this was the seventies, so there were no laws against sexual harassment at the time), and my boyfriend even stepped in to warn the lout to leave me alone. Yet this guy was a classic bully who would not be pushed around. I even went above his head to complain to his supervisor, who turned out to be a card-carrying member of the Good Old Boys Club. He reacted by telling me that I was "lucky to work for such a talented boss." I knew then that it was time to look for another job. One afternoon I was driving home after the principal threatened to fire me if I didn't do what he wanted. I felt an anxiety attack coming on. My heart started racing, my palms became sweaty, and my head felt as if it was about to explode. I quickly pulled the car over to calm my nerves and breathe. When I got home, I called my boyfriend, who came over to comfort me. He went into our fridge and took out my roommate's bottle of wine. At age twenty-four, I still hadn't touched a drop of alcohol, but I was reeling from my day at work.

He placed a sympathetic hand on my shoulder. "Here," he offered. "This will help calm you down."

I drank the foreign substance slowly, savoring each sip. Lo and behold—my anxiety began to fade away. As the alcohol coursed through my bloodstream, my entire body began to relax. The shooting pain in my neck abated, my pulse slowed, and my headache disappeared. I stopped thinking about the unrelenting pressure of my job and for the first time in a year felt "normal."

After that, I started buying wine and going out with friends to drink socially. I would drink a glass of wine (or two or three) almost every day in the evening after work to relieve my anxiety. Even though I was drinking every day, I never became a black-out alcoholic. I rationalized my drinking by believing that I was just like everyone else I knew. For the first time in my life I was one of the gang.

Soon afterward, I was accepted into the doctoral program at Penn State. I felt so elated that I immediately gave notice at my job. As in the movie *The Paper Chase*, I copied my acceptance letter, carefully folded it into a paper airplane, and flew it into the principal's office, silently cheering, "I'm outta here!"

Even though I had left the job that caused me so much stress, my anxiety did not vanish. In fact, during the spring while I prepared to move to Pennsylvania, my anxiety escalated. Even though I was pursuing one of my life's dreams, I continued to drink more and more. At this point I didn't only *want* to drink, I *needed* to drink. It was a subtle change, but I remember it clearly. It went from "Let's go out with the girls for a nightcap" to watching the clock until it was time that I could start drinking again. I was using alcohol to self-medicate.

Now that I have studied alcohol and addiction, I know that my drinking eventually triggered my anxiety attacks. I started to second-guess my decision to move to Pennsylvania. I knew something was wrong with me, but I still didn't realize that it was my alcoholism. My attacks continued to get worse and now occurred on a weekly basis. It was always the same: my pulse would race, my hands would shake, my palms would sweat, and I felt as if someone was sticking a knife in the back of my neck. Despite these physical symptoms, I never considered going to a doctor or a therapist because I would have been embarrassed to confess my troubles to a stranger. I didn't understand that I had an alcohol problem, because the only alcoholic I had ever known was an old friend of the family, who was drunk all of the time, or the homeless people who slept on the street. So I reached for my best friend at the time, which was the bottle. Because alcohol depresses the central nervous system, it quelled my attacks. After a while, I began to drink *before* my attacks to prevent them from coming on. Had I gone to a doctor, I'm sure I would have been given a medication such as valium, but that would have been switching one addiction for another. Because I couldn't control my anxiety attacks, I decided not to go to Penn State. It cost me my doctorate in speech and communications. Instead, I got a job teaching speech and debating at a religious university in a small town in Texas. The school administrators made me sign a contract stating that I wouldn't drink, smoke, or behave in any matter that was morally suspect. I signed, of course knowing I would break that rule, because I just wanted to get on with my life and my career. Yet if you had spoken to any of my colleagues or students at the time, no one had a clue about what I was doing in private. Spiritually, I felt disconnected from God. I had no great aspiration to help others because I could not even help myself. I had no real purpose in life but to survive the next day. All of my dreams of achievement had fallen by the wayside and were replaced with fear, anxiety, guilt, shame, and utter confusion. How did I go from the "top of the heap" to the "bottom of the barrel" in such a short time?

Thankfully, I never drove drunk when taking the debate team on a field trip to a tournament. I'd wait until I was tucked into my hotel room late at night to uncork. The pain I felt then was shame for what I was doing in secret, especially in light of my teaching at a religious institution. Despite my drinking, I did well and was given a promotion. I stayed there for several years. The last year I taught at the school, I was asked me to give the commencement address. I agreed, but I knew, even though I had no fear of public speaking, that I couldn't do it without having a few drinks first. I ended up giving a stirring address while I was under the influence, which is both ironic and shameful. Yet the lesson I learned was that I could drink and get away with it. I was able to do my job, do it well, and still drink. I drank at home, alone, with the drapes closed in my little apartment. I felt desperate, alienated, disenchanted with the world, and afraid of everything. I was scared of failure, being found out, disappointing my parents, disappointing my friends, and not accomplishing what I thought I was supposed to. It felt like being stuck in a maze. Every day I would promise myself to do better and to get it together, and every day I failed to live up to that commitment. Every morning I'd wake up vowing that this day would be different, and every night I would pour another glass of wine and decide that *tomorrow* I would make things right again.

I felt as if the alcohol was keeping me alive emotionally. I was no longer drinking socially because I had broken up with my boyfriend, and I was living in a small town where I hardly knew anyone. My fellow faculty members were all much older than me. I lived isolated from everyone around me for a total of two years until I just couldn't take it anymore. My pain was mental, emotional, social, and spiritual. I was disgusted with myself for abandoning my spiritual and moral beliefs. The only thing I had going for me was my physical health, which was also failing because I started to gain weight, especially in the last few months of my alcoholism.

I decided to quit my university job and move to Dallas, where I got a job as a recruiter for a technology company. I led some communication seminars, which I enjoyed, but my drinking made it difficult for me to continue public speaking. During the last six months that I drank, I was headed toward my bottom. A physical addiction had taken hold. I kept getting headaches and felt nauseated because my body craved the alcohol. At this point, I was drinking not because I *wanted* to but because my body *needed* it to stave off the withdrawal.

On a typical day, I would get up in the morning and have a screwdriver (vodka and orange juice) before going to work. I'd eat lunch in my car by myself, where I would mix vodka in with my Sprite. I was starting to fall apart physically and emotionally. My parents were worried about me, not because they knew I was drinking, but because they could see that I was depressed. Not only was I isolating myself from friends, I stopped coming home for the holidays. My family insisted that I get some medical help. I finally agreed to see a doctor, who asked me whether I drank alcohol, which is a routine question during a physical examination. I lied and said, "The usual amount." Yet he called me a few days later after getting my blood test and said, "I think you are drinking too much. Your enzyme levels in your liver are elevated. You might not think that you are drinking too much, but your body isn't tolerating the alcohol well, so cut back."

I feigned surprise and agreed to cut back. He asked me to call him in a few weeks. I was frightened by what the doctor said, which only added to my shame and anxiety. That was my first revelation that I had a drinking problem. I was now twenty-eight, and after four years of drinking I thought that I couldn't stop. I wanted to stop, but I just couldn't. I didn't know how. "What's wrong with me?" I asked God. "Why am I drinking every day?" I prayed for answers. I was tired of fighting. I was tired of fighting the shame and the guilt.

My Recovery

What alcoholics like us have in common is that we consider alcohol the acceptable means of coping with situations we find uncomfortable or unbearable. It's a lot easier to pour a glass of wine than it is to see a therapist or a clergy member or to look deep inside yourself to discover what is driving you to drink. Alcohol is a friend you call on when you feel ill equipped to handle things yourself.

The tipping point for me was the day one of my college sorority sisters came to town for a visit. When I opened the door, she took one look at me and said, "My God, what has happened to you!?" I had gained thirty pounds, even though I had stopped eating, and I looked a mess. Her reaction prompted me to break down crying, and I spilled out my story to her. My friend, who also knew my sister, called her to say how worried she was about me. My sister immediately alerted our parents. Within a week, my father showed up at my house. That was on Father's Day 1979. He said, "We're worried about you. We know something is wrong, and we want to help you."

I was at a loss for what to say. I didn't want to admit that I was an alcoholic, so instead I said, "I think Betty Ford and I have something in common."

Somehow, having a woman of her stature come out about her alcoholism made it easier for me to admit my own problem. I've always been grateful to her for that, and later in my career as a recovery counselor I had the opportunity to tell her in person when she came to Texas Tech to speak at the university. I was hosting a reception for her at my house, and I told her that she helped me give a voice to what I was struggling with.

Finally, I decided to do the right thing. I took a leave of absence from my job, packed my bags, and signed myself into a medical treatment center the next day. I didn't tell a soul where I was going. I was afraid to go because I didn't know whether I was going to be locked in a room to sweat it out, similar to a scene from *The Lost Weekend*, or what was going to happen. As it turned out, I loved treatment! It was like an awakening for me. The first two days I was given medication to help me withdraw from the alcohol. (Alcohol is one of the most dangerous substances to detox from because withdrawal can actually produce seizures.) After the third day, I woke up feeling great. It had been so long since I had actually woken up without any chemicals in my system. This was one incentive for me to stay sober. I looked forward to each day. My head was clear, and I was happy for the first time in years. Part of the reason my mood was so elevated was because I hadn't been ingesting a depressive drug.

I went to group and individual therapy, as well as to recovery-oriented meetings. The doctors wanted us to meet someone in the community who might offer to be our sponsor after leaving the treatment center. At the time, I was one of only three women in my group, and I was the youngest and most educated by far. Yet my fellow patients were lovely people, and we formed strong bonds and friendships.

At the hospital, the staff let me continue running (which really helped my recovery). I had been an avid runner, so every morning they discharged me from the hospital and let me run around the nearby park. They needed to fill out a lot of paperwork to allow me to do this, but they never once complained or worried that I was a flight risk. Running was (and still is) one of my greatest coping mechanisms. It helps relieve my anxiety and clears my head whenever I face the bumps and dings of everyday life.

My counselor there was an exceptional person in so many ways. Her name was Irene, but many of us jokingly called her the "Big Book bitch" because she walked and talked the *Big Book*, the official title for which is *Alcoholics Anonymous*, and would quote it chapter and verse. If someone stepped out of line, she'd say, "You'd better read step two again." We were encouraged to read every morning and to say a daily prayer or meditate. I still start every day this way as often as I can.

By following the steps I learned in recovery, I realized that I was sick, why I became sick, and what I needed to do to get well. I read, I listened, and I followed every word. One day, Irene took me into a room where a woman was dying. She lay there, jaundiced from liver damage. Irene introduced me to the woman and told her I was a new patient. I asked her how she was feeling and did my best to comfort her, but inside I was horrified. After we left, Irene turned to me and said, "That could be you someday." That was all it took. Five weeks later I was discharged from treatment. After I got out, there were times, I admit, when I thought, "A small glass wine isn't going to hurt me." Yet I remembered what Irene had said and pictured that dying woman and knew that I needed to treat my disease seriously. Alcoholism is chronic, which means you can never be fully "cured." It stays with you for the rest of your life. I wondered, however, whether my anxiety would go away so that I wouldn't have a desire to drink again. It didn't go away immediately, but I learned how to manage it in healthier ways. I never took medication, for example, after my initial detox. Even after I broke my shoulder last year and underwent surgery, I asked the doctor to treat me with as few painkillers as possible. I didn't want to substitute one addiction for another. I continue to have a very healthy respect for the disease of addiction.

I decided that I would choose life over alcohol. My discharge planner suggested that I not return to Dallas, where I had no support network for my recovery, and to pursue my doctorate at Texas Tech in Lubbock instead, which is where I am now. Penn State was just too far away from the recovery contacts whom I had met in Texas. By the time I got out of treatment, I had a group of friends who were recovering alcoholics, and support groups, as you will learn, are essential to the recovery process.

I was discharged in July and started my doctorate in August. I switched my studies from communications to human development and family studies, with a focus in addiction. I had found my calling, and my communications degree helps me to spread the message through education and counseling. I got a teaching fellowship and began to study alcoholism in families and adolescents. One day the hospital where I had been treated called me about a fifteen-year-old girl who was a full-blown alcoholic. She had just checked in, and the hospital staff member asked me whether I would talk to her. We got her into a recovery program, and I became her mentor. While working with this girl, I discovered that teenagers use alcohol as their coping mechanism during adolescence—a subject that became my dissertation and specialty.

Sadly, out of the fifteen people I was with in rehab, I was the only one who made it. One relapsed after six weeks. Another made it a year and a half before drinking again. The counselors warned us that potentially only one out of the group would make it, which is a horrifying statistic. Why was I so successful when others weren't? Why was I able to stop drinking? People think they are different—that they can do it on their own—but it's about learning new and better ways to cope with your pain, which I hope this book will show you how to do. I used exercise, talk therapy, meditation, prayer, and the support of friends, family, and mentors to help me cope with my pain and nurture my recovery.

I also listened to what the experts told me to do. If you do what the counselors and the recovery literature tell you, if you follow the suggestions—it works. If you talk to people who have relapsed, they'll tell you that they quit going to recovery meetings or stopped having quiet time or reading the recovery literature. I also maintained a strong spiritual foundation that continues to support me to this day. And every time I see an alcoholic, I say, "There but for the grace of God . . ."

Another thing that helped me was forming a social network, a community that values similar principles. I don't hide from alcohol. Many of my friends and family members continue to drink. To balance that out, though, I also surround myself with people in recovery. My husband, for example, who was never a drinker, and I live a happy, sober life together. I took a hard fall, but I developed the skills that allowed me to get up again. I'd love to say that I was smart or special, but the truth is that I had the grace of God, a supportive family, healthy relationships, a successful career, and a wonderful recovery program, all of which helped me get back on my feet again.

I also found a sponsor, and I followed her advice. She had been sober twelve years when I met her. If she had told me I needed to crawl down the highway on my hands and knees to stay sober, you would have seen me crawling out on the road. It is about having the desire and the will to live a better life than you have now and finding someone who can show you how to do that. This is why treatment centers often hire people who are in recovery. If a facility's employees haven't experienced the pain of addiction, patients will say, "You don't know what I've been through." It's similar to veterans who can identify only with those who have seen combat.

After getting my doctorate, I worked at a psychiatric hospital for thirteen years as the director of its adolescent substance abuse program. Later I went into private practice, working with women and families who had issues with addiction. I was happy with my work and with my life, but an administrator at Texas Tech University approached me about running the school's center for addiction and recovery. He said, "You touch people every hour several times a day in therapy. If you come here, you can reach hundreds and thousands of people."

That was all it took. I quit my practice and went to Texas Tech, where I have been the director of the Center for the Study of Addiction and Recovery for the last ten years. At the time, it was one of only three in the United States. Now we have twenty programs at other universities around the country. We have a national database for research and a national foundation for collegiate recovery, which we share with other colleges. My goal is to have a collegiate recovery community in at least one college in every state, where thousands of students can learn how to stay clean and sober while continuing their education.

This is my thirty-second anniversary of sobriety, so I feel as if I've come full circle, from being a young graduate struggling with addiction to helping others live the best lives they can. It is about second chances. If you made a bad choice, you don't have to live with it the rest of your life. My hope is that you or someone you love will have a second chance, which I got and which everyone deserves. I believe with all of my heart that if you want to sober up, you can do so as long as you get with the program, whatever program you choose. Whether it's twelve steps or another program, twelve step–focused or not, it doesn't matter as long as it works for you. I promise that anyone who embraces humility, gratitude, and a willingness to do whatever it takes to stay sober will never touch another drop of liquor and will live the life he or she was put on this earth to live.

2

Where Does It Hurt?

"The art of life is the art of avoiding pain."
—*Thomas Jefferson*

P ain is universal. I have yet to meet a woman (or a man) who hasn't experienced it at some point in her life. Whether it's a physical illness, depression, or the loss of a job or a loved one, the type of pain we feel depends on our personal history and circumstances. Although pain afflicts all of us, regardless of age, gender, race, creed, color, or economic status, what separates people who have a drinking problem from those who don't is how we choose to cope with whatever hurts us. Some women use therapy, charity, exercise, hobbies, work, family, or friends to help them through the tough times—others turn to the bottle.

Alcohol undoubtedly gives us initial relief from pain. Drinking a glass of wine or a martini after a long, hard day will help us relax. Most alcoholic women, myself included, started by drinking socially. Alcohol is a lot like dessert; it is great to indulge in every now and then if you can, but if you use a substance to dull the pain, relieve stress, or fill a void in your life, you are eventually going to have a problem. You might not wake up the next morning and find yourself three hundred pounds heavier or a raging alcoholic, but you could be gradually descending into a cycle of compulsive behavior.

This chapter is about the compulsive cycle of alcoholism, which is fueled by pain. It doesn't matter what kind of pain you are experiencing in your life, because whatever it is, it contributes to your desire to drink. Alcohol will temporarily make you feel normal again, but when that fades away—and it eventually will—the stress or anxiety will return, and you will want to drink again. If your drinking continues, you are bound to experience negative consequences. These can include neglecting yourself, your spouse or partner, or your children. Your friends (at least, those who aren't drinking buddies) will stop calling. You will show up late for work or start to make mistakes. Maybe you'll be fired.

If you're still in school, your grades will slip, and you might drop out. As your relationship or marriage crumbles, you might get divorced or even lose custody of your kids. Some women get DUIs and go to prison, alienating themselves even further from their community and society. If the drinking goes on long enough, you could get an alcohol-related illness such as liver damage, diabetes, or cancer.

Of course, these negative consequences produce a tremendous amount of guilt and shame, especially for women. Unlike men, women tend to blame themselves for their alcohol abuse. A man might say, "If you worked as hard as I do, you'd drink, too." I'm not saying that all women are ashamed of their behavior, but it's still more acceptable for a man to kick back at a bar with the boys than it is for a woman. As the primary caregivers, women need to be home in time to make dinner or pick up the kids from school. When they fall down on the job as mothers, there is a domino effect of people who are taken down with them. This humiliation creates even more pain for many women—and around and around we go.

THE CORE RECOVERY PROCESS

This book explains a universal process that all alcoholics, especially women, experience in the course of their addiction and recovery. I call it the Core Recovery Process model, which includes both the compulsive cycle and the coping cycle.

The compulsive cycle works something like this: the guilt and shame we feel from the negative consequences of drinking will feed and exacerbate the pain. The more pain you have, the more you will drink—and the more you drink, the more negative consequences you will experience. The more negative consequences happen, the more guilt, shame, and pain you feel. Nonalcoholics often wonder why people don't simply stop drinking once the negative consequences occur. Well, some do. Yet if you stop drinking without addressing your pain, you are not dealing with what caused you to drink in the first place. It's like sprinkling water on a fire. The chances of putting out the flames are slim.

This is what keeps people stuck in the compulsive cycle. It is why the relapse rate is so high in treatment centers that deal only with the behavior. It is difficult to identify what's driving the compulsive cycle in just twenty-eight days, the average rehab stay. The talented and troubled actress Lindsay Lohan, who has been through a revolving door of rehabs, is a famous example of an addict who is not dealing with her pain. In Lindsay's case, it seems to result from a dysfunctional family with a history of alcoholism.

By examining the motivation behind the behavior, rather than focusing solely on the drinking itself, you have a greater chance of recovering. Drinking is only a *symptom*. It is vital, therefore, to identify what your pain is, be it fresh or decades old, and to find another, healthier way to deal with what hurts, other than dulling it with alcohol.

The Five Types of Pain

Once I had an epiphany while teaching a class on addiction and recovery. I realized that pain is the catalyst that causes compulsive behavior. It led me to develop my Core Recovery Process (CRP) model, the model for recovery that has helped hundreds of people get and stay sober, which I will discuss in part two of this book. As I mentioned earlier, we must treat the pain that causes the addiction, rather than the shame that fuels it. If you approach the alcoholic by shaming her (by saying, for example, "Look what you are doing to yourself and to your family!"), it will only cause her more pain and guilt, which keeps her mired in the cycle of addiction. Too often, well-meaning family, friends, and even recovery experts focus on getting the alcoholic to stop her behavior (in this case, drinking), rather than helping eliminate the pain that causes the behavior in the first place. After years of working with alcoholics, I found five categories of pain that women typically experience, and I've described them here.

1. Physical Pain

"The greatest evil is physical pain."
—*Saint Augustine*

There is no doubt that alcohol can help alleviate physical pain. It was used by soldiers in the field when there was no anesthetic available. It works by suppressing the central nervous system, which can help with chronic diseases such as fibromyalgia, headaches and migraines, arthritis, back pain, PMS (see "The National Association of Premenstrual Syndrome [NAPS]," in the sidebar), or menstrual cramps.

Nancy, a single mother in her late thirties, began to self-medicate with alcohol before she was officially diagnosed with the autoimmune disease lupus. Alcohol helped relieve her aching muscles and joints. Although drinking eased her symptoms, she eventually got to the point where she couldn't get out of bed in the morning to go to work. She blamed her frequent absences on the lupus, but her employer soon suspected that alcohol was causing her debilitation. She finally went into recovery after seeing a doctor, who encouraged her to stop drinking and prescribed appropriate medication.

The aches and pains of aging are one reason older women increasingly turn to alcohol. According to the National Institute for Alcohol Abuse and Alcoholism (NIAAA), elderly patients are admitted to hospitals nearly as often for alcohol-related causes as for heart attacks. Older women are especially sensitive to the stigma of alcoholism, which makes them reluctant to admit that they have a drinking problem. To make matters worse, older women reach higher levels of blood alcohol faster than younger women who drink the same amount, due to a reduction in the body's water content as we age.

THE NATIONAL ASSOCIATION OF PREMENSTRUAL SYNDROME (NAPS)

Until recently, I didn't know that this organization, which is based in the United Kingdom, existed, yet its website features a number of women who confessed to drinking when they were in hormonal distress. If you suffer from PMS, please visit this site before you reach for that lager.

> I was wondering if anyone had any problems with alcohol control during PMS? I have noticed that this is becoming an issue with me. I have been to see the doctor, and he has prescribed norithisterone for my mood swings. I suffer from irritability, anxiety, and weepiness a few days before my period. I also get hunger pangs and chocolate cravings. But the alcohol is my biggest worry, as I cannot seem to stop myself having a drink at this time of the month. I drink moderately at other times. Is it just me?
>
> —Suzano

> I know that alcohol is supposed to have a negative effect on PMS, but I found that up to last year, I was drinking more in a bid to try to calm down my moodiness. When PMSing and irritable, I'd start at about 4 p.m., so I was still able to be in control of the kids till hubby got home at 6 p.m. It did chill me out, actually. Hubby could be in the door for hours before I started at him over nothing much! I've always been a happy drunk, not an aggressive one (when on nights out!), but starting at Weight Watchers stopped me doing that as much. I definitely put lots of weight on due to the increased drinking!

I'd also go around to a girlfriend's house at lunchtime, do a bottle of wine, stagger happily to the school pickup (not far from friend's house), and go back for another bottle while kids played together. Then hubby would get a call at work asking him to get off the bus at my friend's to drive us all home. (God, when I read that back, it sounds awful!) I found I was calmer, chilled, and definitely less irritable . . . but obviously worrying when in charge of young children. Scary, actually, but on bad PMS days it was the only thing that got me through the irrational anger at the world. I know it just masked the symptoms, so not a good idea, but some days, masking was good enough for me!

—Clare

2. Mental Pain

"The pain of the mind is worse than the pain of the body."
—Publilius Syrus, Roman author, first century BCE

Although physical pain can be debilitating, mental (or psychological) pain is the number-one reason women drink. Clinical depression affects twelve million American women each year, according to the Mental Health America, and approximately one in eight women can expect to suffer from depression at some point during her life. According to studies, women are nearly twice as likely as are men to struggle with depression, which can occur at any age but most commonly occurs between the ages of twenty-five and forty-four. The causes of female depression and even the patterns of symptoms, however, are often different from those of male depression. Some factors that contribute to depression in women include hormones, infertility, postpartum blues, and family stress. Women who are bipolar (with moods that swing from manic highs to depressive lows) will frequently self-medicate with alcohol during the hyper stage in order to calm down. The problem with treating depression by drinking is that alcohol is a depressant drug. You might feel better temporarily, but when the effects wear off, you will crash and burn. I like to say that you are chasing your depression with alcohol, which will inevitably make your depression worse.

This was the case with my drinking—the more I drank, the more depressed I got.

Increased Demands on Women

Although depression might be foremost in the hierarchy of mental pain, anxiety is a close second. I see more women with anxiety disorders than ever before. One reason is that women are juggling many more duties nowadays, with the combination of work and family obligations. Expectations for what women can and should achieve have also increased over the years, causing an enormous amount of anxiety in their lives. That was the case for me. The high expectations I placed on myself were the main cause for my anxiety and therefore of my drinking.

Despite the economic downturn, the number of working women in the United States will reach nearly seventy-six million by 2014, according to the AFL-CIO Department for Professional Employees, with the most dramatic increase among wives. Most mothers today, even those with young children, work outside the home, and before they go off to work, they must dress, feed, and prepare their children for school. It is no surprise that so many working women find it difficult to maintain their mental health. Ask any mother how she feels after putting in a full day at work, cleaning the house, cooking hot meals, checking homework, and squeezing in an hour of "me time," either at the gym or reading (if possible!)—all before she turns in for the night. Yet millions of women do this every day. This harried work/home schedule can take a toll on a woman's mental health. Many women who try to juggle jobs and family tell me they drink because they are afraid that people will discover that they aren't the superwomen they pretend to be. Although technology has made our lives easier in terms of having access to information, being wired has also put women on call 24/7. Unlike using alcohol as a remedy for depression, drinking to quell anxiety actually works. If you feel anxious about something and you have a glass of wine, you're going to feel better. The problem is that you might wake up in the middle of the night because your central nervous system is craving this antianxiety drug. Once again, the bang that alcohol gives you for your buck is only temporary. It feeds into the compulsive cycle of dependence and will eventually make your anxiety worse.

I Was Living with a Chemical Lobotomy

Forty-seven-year-old Andrea talks about being bipolar
and an alcoholic.

I didn't know I was bipolar until I was in treatment. I started drinking when I was a teenager because it was the cool thing to do. My alcoholism didn't progress rapidly, but the older I got, the worse it got. I have what's called hypomania, which means I live in the upside without the lows. Unlike other bipolars, I didn't drink during low periods, I drank *all the time*. Hypomanic people like me don't need much sleep, and we tend to be outgoing, competitive, and have lots of energy. We are fully functional and are often extremely productive. This is why I won a national teaching award, even while drinking. The mania helps you to be successful, so it's a hard disease to detect.

When my brain was up, I'd drink as a mood stabilizer. Bipolar people are willing to take more risks, so you drink more. I had been taking Zoloft, a medication for depression, which was one of the worst things you can do if you are bipolar. I felt like I was living with a chemical lobotomy.

When I was at my worst, I would spend days at a hotel so I could drink by myself. I would hide pints of vodka in my car and pick up boxes of wine every few days, so no one knew how much I was drinking. I nearly lost my teaching job when my supervisor smelled alcohol on my breath at one of our meetings. My husband, who served in Afghanistan (another reason to drink), finally got together with a friend of mine and took me to rehab.

I've been sober since 2008, and my bipolar condition is under control, thanks to a nurse practitioner who is constantly adjusting my medications. Treatment, AA, my family, and my doctors have all helped me get and stay sober. I've connected with new friends who have common goals, and I am constantly reminding myself that I am an alcoholic, especially when I start feeling like I'm all better. I want other women who have a drinking problem to remember that life is not manageable sometimes. You aren't God—you can't manage everything. Take it one day at a time, and, as time goes by, it just gets better and better.

3. Emotional Pain

> "Painful as it may be, a significant emotional event can be the catalyst for choosing a direction that serves us—and those around us—more effectively. Look for the learning."
>
> —*Louisa May Alcott, author*

Emotional pain encompasses everything from disappointment, rejection, and loss to anger and fear. Whatever the cause, women are still not allowed to express their full range of emotions. We are supposed to be perennially cheerful and supportive. When a man at the office blows up, it's fine, but if a woman does the same thing, she's labeled a bitch. When a woman is rejected in a relationship or a marriage, this often causes her an enormous amount of emotional distress.

Divorced women are especially prone to drinking, because many single women still go to bars to find a man. The guilt and shame they feel about being divorced and the social anxiety of finding someone who will love them again increase their desire to drink. If a woman is left for a younger or prettier woman, she has an additional crisis of confidence. When a woman tries to date while raising children, this intensifies her fear that she is not doing the best that she can for her family.

Whether you are dealing with a new pain, such as divorce, or an old pain that you experienced as a child, it needs to be addressed. Maybe you never got the love and recognition you deserved from your parents. Perhaps you were sexually abused.

This is what I call family-of-origin pain. Dealing with family history, no matter how long ago it occurred, is no less raw than the pain you might feel at the moment. In fact, it often takes longer to recover from childhood pain because it has been festering for so long. Yet unless or until it is dealt with, it will not go away.

Women who are physically or verbally abused by a spouse or a partner experience myriad types of emotional pain. Not only are they afraid for their safety and well-being, they are often isolated by their abusers, have low or no self-esteem, and are deeply hurt by the rejection they experience from the abusers and other family members who are either complicit or simply look the other way. Ask any woman who has been abused, and she will tell you that she is filled with pain, shame, and guilt—pain that comes from the abuse, shame for being in this position in the first place, and guilt for not having the emotional fortitude to leave. If you or someone you know is in this situation, and there are thousands, you must gather together your personal effects and your children, if you have them, and find someplace safe where you can get help.

I Thought Alcoholics Were People Who Slept under Bridges

Helen, fifty-nine, recounts her thirty-year struggle with alcohol.

I started drinking when I was twenty-one after my boyfriend gave me a beer. I loved it so much that I drank the whole six-pack, which made me sick all night. I had served liquor as a waitress, but I had never tried it because I'm pretty straitlaced. My parents didn't drink, and I had never been around drinkers, so I thought that alcoholics were people who slept under bridges. That's how naive I was. I didn't drink again for another five years after I married a physically and emotionally abusive man. He would wake me up in the middle of the night and call me a whore. He would also wake up our three-year-old and say, "Tell your mommy she's a whore!" The abuse got progressively worse as he became more and more controlling.

I started drinking again when my husband wasn't around because I couldn't handle his condemnation and disapproval. I left once to go to a shelter, but my friends at the time were members of our fundamentalist church, where my husband also worked, and they convinced me to go back. Not long after that, I left him for good. He stalked me for a while, but I knew that I had to leave because he was teaching my son to be abusive.

When my son graduated from high school and left home, I started drinking high-quality Merlot. At one point, I was drinking a bottle of wine a night. I tried to wait until five, so I would watch the clock and then drink myself silly.

The turning point for me was the day I went out to my garage to hide my wine bottle in the trunk and noticed that the seat was fully reclined. The keys were in the ignition and the garage was locked, which I never do. Apparently, I had blacked out the night before and tried to kill myself, but I couldn't remember what had happened. It scared me so much that I Googled "alcoholism" and got the name of an AA meeting that was ten minutes from where I live in southern Oregon. I drove there immediately to ask if I was an alcoholic.

I truly believe God got me to that meeting. Five women came up to me afterward and asked if I wanted to join them for a soda. They assured me that I was classic alcoholic and that it would only get worse if I continued drinking. I said, "Where do I sign?" I started going to thirteen meetings a week, and I haven't had a drop of alcohol since. Every day was a struggle, especially for the first three months. But I didn't want to give my son an alcoholic mother after everything else he had been through. If it wasn't for him, I'm not sure I would have stopped. I haven't had a drink in three years.

4. Social Pain

"Yes, they're sharing a drink they call loneliness.
Well, it's better than drinking alone."
—Billy Joel, "The Piano Man"

Social pain is the feeling that you don't fit in or that no one understands you. It is the feeling of isolation that can be brought on by being left out of cliques at school, being shunned or ridiculed for being different, or by having a negative self-image or bad feelings about your body. It is an indisputable fact that women are held to a higher standard of attractiveness than men are, so if you think you are ugly or not pretty *enough*, you will probably feel socially uncomfortable. Obesity is extremely painful, especially for women who see being thin as the physical ideal. Being excluded or ridiculed by bullies, which happens most often in middle school and high school, is another form of social violence. According to a survey of playgrounds reported by Stop Bullying Now, a bullying incident in the United States occurs once every seven minutes. Victims often feel alienated and alone. Some "mean girl" tactics include making prank calls or sending harassing e-mails; playing jokes or "punks" that are designed to embarrass or humiliate; whispering with other kids, with the intention of making the victim feel left out; name-calling and spreading malicious gossip among peers; gaining a person's trust, then turning against her; encouraging others to pick on a specific target; and inciting others to act out violently or aggressively. As we have seen in the incidents of suicide by young victims of bullies, being socially harassed can be as painful as a physical assault.

Another less painful, yet pervasive, social malaise is boredom, which can frequently lead to alcoholism. If you live in a small town where there isn't a lot to do, alcohol is a common and accessible form of entertainment. When I ask teenagers why they started drinking, they frequently answer, "There's nothing else to do."

When a girl is smarter than her peers in high school, she will sometimes drink to relieve her intellectual tedium. For older women, leaving the workplace to have a family can be socially isolating. The lack of mental stimulation during the child-rearing years has created a new category of female alcoholics called mom-tini mothers, which I discuss in chapter 6.

Ultimately, all female alcoholics with social pain share one emotion: loneliness. People often think that drinking is something that happens at a bar, a club, or a party, but for women who are closet drinkers, one of their greatest fears is being found out. I am an excellent example of this. I never went to bars to drink. I always did my drinking at home, alone.

At 37 I Had Come to Believe That My Best Years Were behind Me

The following testimony was posted on www.mysobernotes.com, which bills itself as "an anonymous place to exchange notes about alcoholism and addiction, meet sober friends and build your recovery network." This blog is filled with stories from recovering alcoholics, such as the following one by Sugamags, who had this to say about feeling isolated.

At 37 I had come to believe that my best years were behind me and that decades of isolation and misery were all I had to look forward to. I thought the best companionship I could ever hope for was that of the canine variety (while I adore my dog, she still is no substitute for human contact), and that I would die a lonely death in the poorhouse with no loved ones to see me through to the end as, naturally, I will never find a mate and fail to produce a family of my own.

As my addiction wore on these fears of a cursed future took hold of my mind and became convictions. They were yet another rationale for my continued substance abuse. "If this is as good as it gets," I told myself, "I might as well take some relief in the only place where I can find it." I told myself that if other people were as unhappy as I was, they'd naturally drink too. The problem in my mind was that most folks just didn't understand real pain like mine. Talk about self-centered thinking!

5. Spiritual Pain

> "Only through experiences of trial and suffering can the soul be strengthened, vision cleared, ambition inspired and successes achieved."
>
> —*Helen Keller*

When I mention spiritual pain, I'm not talking about religion. Spiritual pain is the feeling that you don't have a sense of purpose or a mission in life. Sometimes it is a loss of faith, especially after tragic events such as the death of a loved one, natural disasters, accidents, foreclosures, or a life-threatening illness. Women who are in spiritual pain feel hopeless. The hardest cases I've had to deal with are those in which a woman loses a child. When this happens, it is difficult to help her find a reason to recover. Widows are prone to drink to fill the huge emptiness in their lives. One woman I know started drinking heavily after her husband died. She continued to drink daily until she passed away at age ninety-four. You don't have to suffer a monumental tragedy, however, to feel lost and not have a reason to get up in the morning. Fortunately, I never suffered a tremendous loss, but in the final days of my drinking, it was a struggle for me to get out of bed each morning. Do you ever ask yourself: Who am I? Why me? Why this? Why now? What is my true potential? What is the meaning of life? Does God exist? Why is life so unfair? Science and even religion often fail to give satisfactory answers to many of these questions. Research shows that women suffer more than men do from spiritual crises. We all need to have a purpose in life and to feel that we are here to be of service or to contribute something to the world. It is this desire to feel *significant*, as opposed to being successful, that creates our spiritual angst. When you get counseling in a treatment center, the focus is usually on how you are doing medically. You can eliminate the body's dependence on alcohol in a hospital, but if you ignore the spiritual pain, you are missing a huge piece of the puzzle that leads to recovery. I call this band-aid therapy. I believe that one reason Alcoholics Anonymous has been so successful is because of the spiritual component in the twelve-step program, which resonates with people who are spiritually lost.

As one AA member put it, "Had I been able to explain to a psychiatrist the feelings of futility, loneliness, and lack of purpose that had come with my deep sense of personal failure, I seriously doubt that the good doctor couldn't have convinced me that my basic problem was a spiritual hunger."

Quiz: Identify Your Pain

One of the first questions I ask female alcoholics is "What is it that hurts so badly?" It might be a combination of the types of pain I mentioned, or it could be all five of them. Once you identify your pain, you can begin to break the cycle, and then you can move on to the next step in the Core Recovery Process. Putting a name to a hurt will help you address it and find healthier ways to deal with all of your feelings without taking a drink.

Take the following quiz to see if you can identify the pain that you have experienced.

1. Are you frequently in some kind of physical pain?
2. Do you suffer regularly from headaches or migraines?
3. Do you get irritable before and during your period?
4. Have you been diagnosed with a chronic disease or illness?
5. Do you have trouble walking?
6. Are you extremely underweight or obese?
7. Do you get hot flashes and night sweats?
8. Do you feel sad most of the time?
9. Have you ever contemplated suicide?
10. Do your moods often fluctuate from extremely high to plunging lows?
11. Have you lost interest or pleasure in activities you used to enjoy?
12. Do you have trouble sleeping at night?

13. Do you have difficulty concentrating?
14. Have you had a sudden change of appetite?
15. Have you been verbally insulted or physically assaulted?
16. Were you sexually abused as a child?
17. Are you estranged from your parents or siblings?
18. Do you feel bored at home, in the workplace, or at school?
19. Did your husband or partner leave you?
20. Do you often fantasize about getting revenge on someone who has slighted you?
21. Do you feel as though you never get a fair shake in life?
22. Are you embarrassed about the way you look?
23. Do you feel as if no one understands you?
24. Are you being bullied or harassed at school or at work?
25. Would you rather stay home alone than go out to parties or other social gatherings?
26. Do you find it difficult to meet new people?
27. Do you feel as if you are different from everyone else?
28. Do you have trouble maintaining friendships or romantic relationships?
29. Do you feel as if your life has no meaning or purpose?
30. Has there been a tragedy in your life?
31. Has someone close to you passed away?
32. Do you sometimes feel that you are unworthy of success or happiness?
33. Have you lost your faith in God or in a higher power?
34. Are you plagued with a feeling of hopelessness?

Answers

Physical Pain (1–7): If you answered "yes" to one or more of the first seven questions, then you are in physical pain. If the cause has not yet been diagnosed by a doctor, I suggest that you see a physician. If you don't have a personal physician, ask someone you trust for references. Similar to my friend with lupus who was unaware of her disease, you need to get the proper treatment to alleviate your discomfort or eliminate the problem so you that don't self-medicate with alcohol or drugs.

Mental Pain (8–14): If you answered "yes" to one or more of these questions, you may be suffering from what I call mental pain. As I mentioned earlier, mental pain is one of the most common reasons women turn to alcohol for comfort. It is often difficult to self-diagnose because you know *something* is wrong, but you can't always put your finger on the problem. Sleepless nights, mood swings, and changes in appetite are red flags that might indicate a more serious psychological problem. If you experience a number of these symptoms or have suicidal thoughts, you need to get professional help (see the Resources at the back of the book for help locating a mental health provider in your area).

Emotional Pain (15–21): If you are being abused by a parent, a spouse, a partner, or a relative; if you've been left by a spouse or a partner; or if you feel as though the world is against you, you are in emotional pain. Feelings of disappointment, alienation, or rejection are all types of emotional pain. Make no mistake, emotional pain can hurt as much as, if not more than, physical pain. As with mental distress, alcohol will help dull your feelings at first, but emotional pain needs to be treated with talk therapy or a combination of therapy and doctor-prescribed medications, if necessary.

Social Pain (22–28): If you answered "yes" to one or more of these questions, you are experiencing social pain, which can affect anyone at any age but occurs more frequently when we are older. For this type of pain, which is marked by loneliness and isolation, telling someone whom you trust what's going on in your life is the first step toward getting help. Make it a point to find places to connect with other people, such as civic clubs, houses of worship, PTA meetings, or volunteer organizations. A great way to remedy social pain is by helping others.

Spiritual Pain (29–34): If you answered "yes" to one or more of these questions, you are having a spiritual crisis. Having a loss of faith or a crisis of confidence in oneself and one's purpose in life, what the French call raison d'être ("reason for being"), is one of the most difficult kinds of pain to treat because it is so deeply profound and personal. I recommend that those in spiritual pain consult a clergy person or a therapist or join a support group such as Alcoholics Anonymous or Al-Anon or another organization with members who will understand what you are going through and will help you to find out what your passion and purpose in life are.

3

Closet Drinkers

ee is a typical thirty-eight-year-old working mother from Ohio who loves her husband and family. Although being a store manager can be stressful at times, she likes her colleagues and the challenges of her job. Yet on most evenings after a long day at work, she comes home and pours herself two or three glasses of red wine, careful to space them out over the evening. When the guilt sets in, she makes herbal tea, convincing herself that the organic properties will offset the alcohol that she continues to, in her words, "guzzle."

"I feel this is more of a habit than an addiction," Lee explains, "but I have a family history of alcoholism, and it terrifies me that I'm going the same way. I suffer from bouts of depression, and I'm trying to make excuses for why I drink, but at the end of the day they're just excuses. I just want to find a happy medium, where I don't feel guilty and I can start enjoying my life to the max. I feel like I'm stuck in a rut!"

Lee, who can tick off every item on the checklist for the compulsive cycle of alcoholism (family history, depression, denial, guilt) is a classic closet drinker. What she probably doesn't realize is that her story is not unusual and that she belongs to a large group of women who drink. The closet drinker, as the moniker describes, is the woman who drinks secretly. She waits until her kids are safely tucked into bed and her husband is otherwise engaged to sneak into the pantry for her private party. No one is the wiser.

The closet drinker tends to be, but is not exclusively, middle-aged and beyond and, unlike her younger counterparts, does not like to drink outside the home. These women are more concerned about the consequences of driving under the influence, or they are professional women who can't afford to be seen in bars, where they could get a bad reputation. Similar to Lee, they are more likely to polish off a bottle of wine alone, when they get home from work. They are also known as functional alcoholics.

Functional alcoholics are able to get by because they appear to be completely in control of their lives. They lead double lives, with each woman having a public face and a private one. Part of the closet drinker mystique is that at least for a while, she is able to do her job or get the kids off to school while drinking. This is what makes it possible to keep her secret from her spouse and family. I was an uncharacteristically young closet drinker who was able to keep my drinking under wraps—until I got caught. And we all eventually do get caught.

Some women, such as Lee, wait until they get home from work before uncorking. Others drink throughout the day. The old saying that "It's five o'clock somewhere in the world" applies to them. The reason some alcoholics can wait to drink at night is because alcohol stays in your system for about thirty-six hours. If you've been drinking in the evening, you are not completely sober the next morning, which is why you won't crave alcohol again until later. Women who drink during the day learn exactly how much it takes to maintain the buzz that they need to get by.

The closet drinker experiences physical, emotional, mental, social, and spiritual pain. She might have empty nest sadness. Some are divorced, are in bad marriages, or are disillusioned with their transition into midlife. They find themselves at forty-five having lost or never found their raison d'être. This is the spiritual pain. Unlike binge drinkers and the barhoppers, whose drinking is part of their social lives, these women drink in isolation. It is their shameful secret.

The one thing I frequently hear from the closet drinker is, "If only people knew who I *really* am." They are ashamed that their lives are circling the drain, and there is no one they feel they can reach out to for help. It is similar to the pain that many gay people feel about hiding a huge part of their identity—thus the "closet" part of the equation. The compulsive cycle that drives them to drink is the shame they feel for what they are doing.

For many closet drinkers, the drink of choice is wine. Think about it. How many women do you see doing shots of whiskey? These women can leave the bottle out on the table without anyone questioning their behavior. One can be a raging alcoholic and drink only the finest, most expensive vintages. Of course, many women do move on to harder liquor, such as vodka, which they can hide in plastic makeup bottles or empty vinegar jars. Alcoholic women can be crafty.

As I said earlier, a common misconception is that alcoholism is determined by how much you drink. In truth, it's not the frequency or the amount; it's the loss of control. What happens is that your drinking will eventually produce myriad negative consequences, which I discuss in the next chapter. For every drinker it's a progression, and the closet drinker is no exception. She knows she has a problem, which is why she hides it. Her shame is not so much about the drinking, it's about the secrecy. Drinking alone is not fun. Alcohol is the reward she gives herself for a hard day's work, whether it is taking care of the house or her job. It is her reward for surviving another day. Alcohol medicates whatever pain she is feeling: "Look at all I've done today. Look at how I've sacrificed for my family. I never have any 'me' time." The closet drinker needs an escape, and sitting in front of the TV just doesn't cut it the way a Cutty Sark does.

Coming Out

If you are a closet drinker, the first thing you must do is tell some-one what's going on so you can get some help, whether it's rehab, counseling, AA, or another recovery program. You don't have to do this alone. Once your body has detoxed from the alcohol, you need to replace your former reward system with something else that is equally satisfying. For some women, it might be exercise. For others, it could be a massage or a pedicure. Because being in the closet is so isolating, you must find a group of friends who are sober, social, and supportive. Think the three Ss.

I cannot overestimate the importance of surrounding yourself with friends who will help you maintain your sobriety. Meetings, religious or spiritual groups, professional organizations, gyms, and even taking continuing education courses are all great ways to get out of the house, meet new people, and break your old drinking patterns. Whatever you do, don't join a group that serves alcohol when the members gather. You might reach a point where you can be around others who drink without it being a temptation (it's difficult to live in this world otherwise), but don't make it too dif-ficult for yourself at first. Often, bridge games, sewing circles, and book clubs are simply excuses for women to get together over wine or cocktails, so ask in advance whether it is a dry group before you join.

My Motto Became "Poor Me, Poor Me; Pour Me Another Drink"

Julie tells the story of how low self-esteem and a dysfunctional family fueled her secret drinking as a teenager and beyond.

On the outside, I was the picture of success. College educated, wife and mother, two cars in the garage, and bills paid on time. My family attended church, and no one would have suspected a thing. I never got a DUI (although many times I deserved one). My employers and neighbors, even sometimes my own husband, were clueless about my excessive drinking.

Everything appeared to be fine, but on the inside I was a wreck. I was either drinking or thinking about drinking all the time. I lived in darkness, apart from God. I was frightened, anxious, and full of shame and guilt about my behavior, determined not to become to my children what my mother was to me, while all the time moving in that same direction. My mother's rule was we could drink as much as we wanted as long as we were at home.

It took a while for me to realize that it wasn't normal to start drinking almost daily as a teenager or to have a mother who encouraged it. When I look back, I realize that she needed a drinking partner, and I was a willing participant, as was my older brother. I remember drinking rum and Coke and playing cards with my mother when I was only fourteen or fifteen. My mother even gave me a bracelet with a little charm of a six-pack of beer on it. She thought it was cute that I liked Budweiser and Myers's rum!

So I drank all through high school. In college, I could drink any guy under the table—except my brother. We were always neck and neck. I had an enormous capacity for alcohol, yet I rarely lost control or made a fool of myself. I later learned that a high tolerance was a tell-tale sign of escalating alcoholism, and it proved to be a wonderful way for me to stay in denial because, after all, I wasn't the sloppy drunk. Someone else had the drinking problem, not me.

I had very low self-esteem. I never really grew up, even into my twenties and thirties. I was desperately lonely and depressed. I was cynical and judgmental, full of resentment and self-pity. I was almost always sick and tired. (Translation: hungover!) But I had to pretend that I wasn't. My greatest efforts went into trying to make people believe (and also to make myself believe) that I was normal. Yet I always had a beer in my hand.

My sneaky drinking started when I was young, too. I was the ultimate closet alcoholic. I could hide cans and bottles with the best of them and hide the fact that I'd been drinking (or so I thought). When I graduated from college, my soon-to-be husband and I moved to Colorado, where we married and lived for five years. After my daughter was born, my closet drinking escalated even more. I especially didn't want people to know I was an alcoholic then—a beer in one hand and a baby in the other.

It was during this time that I did try to quit or at least to control my drinking. Countless times I would swear off—but someone would push a beer my way, and I was off and running again. The humiliating incidents were happening more and more. People were starting to notice. My husband was nagging me continually about my drinking, which made me even sneakier.

While pregnant with my son, I somehow stayed sober for those nine months, as was the case with my first pregnancy. But soon after my son was born, I was off to the races again with my drinking. It was then that I crashed and burned and made my first trip into Alcoholics Anonymous. No one in my family had ever gone for help, so I knew nothing about the twelve steps or the spiritual aspect of recovery from alcoholism. I didn't stay long! I wanted to do things my way. I only wanted to go to women's meetings because that was where I felt most comfortable. I didn't want to have a sponsor or get close to anyone. I didn't ask for help in working the steps. I didn't want to share in meetings about what was going on with me. In fact, I was scared to death to share in meetings!

I rationalized that the group was cliquey, and I didn't fit in. I always felt like life was a private club, and everyone knew the password but me. So there I was again—back to my loneliness and isolation, only dry! I was always looking for that elusive sense of comfort that I thought I could find in a bottle, and being sober in the beginning is NOT comfortable. So naturally, I drank again.

My marriage began to crumble around me, so I self-medicated more and more with the booze. It was also during this time that my mother was diagnosed with terminal cancer. I became extremely bitter and resentful toward my husband, convinced that he did not love or support me in my time of need. I was terrified of losing my mother, after having already lost my dad. In retrospect, I realized I had never really grieved his loss; I just drank away the pain, year after year.

I was in such denial about how my alcoholism and codependent ways contributed to the problems in my marriage. All I could see were my *husband's* faults and failings. Now I can see how self-centered and misdirected my thinking was. I was so sure that divorce would solve my problems, but I had no idea what was ahead in terms of a bitter custody battle over my two children. Those were the worst days of my life.

I actually quit drinking for a two-year period (with only a few slips). I was terrified of losing my children. Fear can indeed be a motivator temporarily for the alcoholic. We might stop drinking because of fear of losing our family, our health, a job, a driver's license, or fear of going to jail. But for the "dry" alcoholic, in other words, someone not working a twelve-step recovery program, it is only a matter of time before the next drink.

My soon-to-be ex-husband began dating and ultimately married his female attorney. I ran out of money, and after making some horrible choices too embarrassing for me to mention, I eventually lost custody of my children. I became the weekend parent. I was never so ashamed of myself. I hated my ex-husband and his new wife with a passion, and I hurt deeply for my children. My motto became, "Poor me, poor me; pour me another drink."

During all this time, I managed to advance in my career. I wish I could say the same for my relationships with men. Immediately after my divorce, without giving myself time to heal, I jumped head-first into the first unhealthy relationship that came along! I ignored all the signs of a second failed marriage and married this man who had two children of his own. So there I was, increasingly sick in my alcoholism, missing my children desperately when they were away, and poorly equipped to handle a difficult relationship and a blended family.

This was what finally brought me to my knees, and I haven't had a drink since September 10, 1995. Soon after that, I separated from my second husband. I joined a wonderful church and became an active member of Alcoholics Anonymous. I clung to my newfound sobriety and relationship with the Lord. I learned so much from the teachings of my pastor. I grew spiritually and healed emotionally through working the twelve steps with a sponsor. I read and studied the Bible, especially my Life Recovery Bible. At about two years sober, I answered a call for volunteers to help start a new program at the church called Celebrate Recovery. But best of all, both of my children came to live with me, and we were able to rebuild a wonderful life together.

Leaving the Past Behind

Closet drinkers have been hiding for so long that they often find it difficult to imagine their lives being any other way. You need to separate your past from the present and from the future. The past was shameful, the present can be different, but the future will be magnificent!

It doesn't matter whom you tell when you first come out of the closet, as long as you set yourself free and stop the lying and the lying low. Here are some other coping suggestions for closet drinkers:

- **Rebuild your nest**. One of the biggest triggers for closet drinkers is the empty nest syndrome. When the children leave, these mothers feel as if they've lost their identities, and booze helps them fill that chasm in their lives. Yet just because your kids are gone doesn't mean you can't find others to take their place. Sign up as a volunteer library assistant at your local elementary school. Public schools are in desperate need of extra help, due to overcrowding and draconian cuts in education, so you're doing yourself, the children, and your community a great service by being with and helping the children.
- **Rediscover your purpose**. Lushes have to feel needed and wanted again. One of the best ways you can do this is to stop

having private pity parties and work on rebuilding your self-esteem. You can volunteer at a drug and alcohol center for teens or at a shelter for runaways. Your firsthand experience with substance abuse will give you the street-cred necessary to bond with these kids and empathize with the difficulties of addiction. Homeless shelters and food pantries are also popping up everywhere as a result of our economic downturn. There's nothing like helping others in need to find out just how fortunate we really are.

- **Help out at a nonprofit organization**. If you are a functional alcoholic who is a professional woman, volunteer to do the bookkeeping or other office work at an animal shelter, a medical clinic, or a financial aid center. If you are an interior designer, make over the home or the apartment of someone who is down on her luck. Creative types and writers can offer to write newsletters and press releases or design brochures for nonprofit organizations.

- **Learn something new**. For wealthy wives who drink because they are bored and suffer from emotional or social pain, the empty nest can be excruciating. If you feel intellectually unchallenged, take a continuing education class in a subject that you always wanted to learn but didn't think you had the time or the inclination to pursue. Find a culinary school and learn how to bake or do a perfect *mis en place*; master the latest computer technology; learn how to speak another language, then visit the country where it is spoken to try out your new skills; learn to play an instrument, and invite your friends to a "salon" where guests can showcase their talents.

- **Give yourself a makeover.** The camouflage of the "functional alcoholic" is to dress nicely, act "normally," and keep it together enough so that no one would suspect she has a drinking problem. That is the way I hid my drinking! The nonfunctional lush, however, might let herself go the way a sick cat does. For this kind of lush, the first step might be showering every day, putting on some makeup, coloring your hair, and buying something to wear that makes you feel attractive and able to face the world.

I realize that this is treating the external problem and simply making yourself presentable will not address the internal pain that causes you to drink. I will tell you this, however—I don't know any man who has ever stopped drinking because he's overweight. So, if looking better is a motivation for you to get off the sauce, fix yourself up! Women are so concerned with their appearance that they are less likely to seek help from the outside world if they are embarrassed about the way they look. So, if a trip to the mall or the gym will get you out of your drunken cocoon and into a meeting, then it's another welcome step toward your getting into the coping cycle.

WOMEN FOR SOBRIETY (WFS)

Closet drinkers and other women who drink excessively might want to look into a group called Women For Sobriety, which was founded in 1976 by Jeane Kirkpatrick, the former UN ambassador, after seeking sobriety for herself. It is the first national self-help program for women alcoholics. Kirkpatrick discovered that there were no programs available that dealt specifically with issues faced by female alcoholics, so she started WFS as a way to address women's unique needs.

"Women's recovery needs are quite different from those of the male alcoholic," Ms. Kirkpatrick noted. "Men and women's attitudes and problems have always been different. Not to recognize this is to deny recovery to the thousands."

Women For Sobriety helps women overcome their alcoholism by encouraging emotional and spiritual growth through a new lifestyle. WFS is not affiliated with Alcoholics Anonymous, although members sometimes belong to AA. Its philosophy involves forgetting the past, planning for tomorrow, and living for today. For more information, visit www.womenforsobriety.org, call 215-536-8026, or send an e-mail to newlife@nni.com.

4

Barhopping

At thirty-four, Katie worries that her window for finding a husband is closing. Many of her friends are already coupled off, and, although she loves her public relations job, she feels a huge chasm in her life. She tries the online dating sites, which are fine for meeting men, but her face-to-face chats at local Chicago cafés feel more like job interviews than dates and aren't nearly as much fun as a girls' night out. When she's trawling the bars and the clubs with her friends, she has someone to talk to, should conversations turn dull, and a guaranteed dance partner when the drinks loosen her inhibitions and allow her to shed her natural shyness.

So, every Saturday night she and her best friend Sarah slip into their spiked heels and minis to hit the town. Whenever she enters a bar, the pounding bass of the music and the dim lights make her heart race with anticipation. "Who will I meet tonight?" It is a mystery that is often solved as the sun paints the skyscrapers a glassy orange. One night Katie and Sarah spot two cute guys texting at the bar and edge their way onto nearby stools to order Absolut with cranberry juice. The young men look up from their BlackBerrys and banter flirtatiously about their jobs (traders), funny viral videos, and sports. They ask the women whether they want to try another bar and, after a ladies room caucus, Katie and Sarah agree to hang with them for the evening.

Countless cocktails and three bars later, the two friends join a chorus line of inebriated women high-kicking and belting out songs with booze-soaked abandon. Katie and her "date" later retreat to a corner, where they kiss passionately until he invites her to his apartment. She tells Sarah, who is locked in an embrace with bachelor number two, that she is leaving and will call her in the morning.

Back at his place, they are barely in the door before their clothes are off and they are on the bed. Katie is too drunk to think about protection (he never asks), and when the sex is over, he lights a joint and says, "I'm going back to the bar—wanna come?" It is 2 a.m.

"No, thanks," she says, unable to lift her head from the pillow. Katie hears the door slam as she stares at the ceiling, which is circling like a carousel. Unsure of where she is, she manages to crawl her way to the bathroom, where she throws up—repeatedly.

Feeling slightly better, she manages to put on her clothes and hail a cab. As the car speeds toward home, she realizes that she forgot her purse. Not knowing whether she is capable of walking home, she tells the cab driver that she lost her wallet and asks him to pull over. Seeing her condition, he takes pity on her and drives her to her doorstep. He writes his name and address on the receipt, and she promises to send him a check, but when she finds the receipt the next day, she has forgotten who he is. It must be the guy she slept with last night, she thinks, coaxing her mind to remember the previous evening. Is he the jerk who left her immediately after sex? The cad does call but only to tell her she left her pocketbook behind. During the cab ride back to his place, she is hungover, exhausted, and ashamed. She calls Sarah on her cell phone to exchange stories and try to fill in the missing pieces. The girls laugh about their exploits and make plans to go out again next Saturday.

Back in the nineties, TV's *Sex and the City* gave single women permission to let their chic flag fly in this version of urban female bonding. We watched as the fab four catwalked in impossibly high heels to New York's hippest bars in search of soul mates or one-night stands. Their conversations rang refreshingly true, but they created an illusion that was part exhilaration, part desperation. The foursome made the Cosmopolitan the cocktail du jour for women who bar-hop. Even the name, like the eponymous magazine that launched in the seventies for its newly liberated female audience, evoked the zeitgeist created by the characters who sipped liberally from them.

The fact is, single women in their twenties and thirties look at themselves through the prism of the media, which sets a high bar for how they should live. The *Sex and the City* women were seemingly smart, rich, and stylish, and they all had interesting jobs. Their friendships were based on the female equivalent of Bros Before 'Hos and the knowledge that no matter how bad their dates and relationships were, they could always circle back to their best friends, or BFFs, to toast away their boyfriend blues.

Today, we have other role models for single women who like to party. Celebutantes Paris Hilton and Lindsay Lohan, real-life barhoppers, are famous for little more than their clothes and clubbing (see sidebar). Inexplicably, they are beloved by many young women who dream of waking up with only two burning questions: "What do I wear today?" and "Where will I go tonight?"

Like all female drinkers, the barhoppers represent a transitional stage in a woman's life. In this case, it is the passage from adolescence or college into young adulthood, where women must work to support themselves and, perhaps, search for a companion. Barhoppers have experienced the competition, either in the business world or in the social world, and they know the hoops they must jump through in order to reach their goals. Alcohol makes them feel better about themselves and is a way to anesthetize the pain of loneliness and the spiritual pain that comes from not really knowing yet what their purpose in life is. This was the case for me, which is why I started drinking in my twenties after being out in the work world for a while. Like a female version of Peter Pan, women during this stage can delay their development by abusing alcohol. This delayed maturation in women leads to a Ya-Ya Sisterhood of fellow drinkers who want to get their ya-yas out while they're still unencumbered by children and other grown-up obligations. In 1970, only 7.4 percent of all American thirty- to thirty-four-year-olds were unmarried; today, that number has increased threefold to 22 percent. Because women today are delaying marriage longer, some are quite happy to be single and explore their sexuality during their twenties and early thirties.

Now, I'm not suggesting that going out with the girls on the weekend makes you an alcoholic, but ask yourself the following questions to see whether you might have a drinking problem:

- Does your partying cause you to be late for work in the mornings?
- Do people not want to be around you when you are drunk?
- Do you surround yourself with friends who like to go out, and do you drop friends who don't like to drink?
- Do you find it increasingly uncomfortable to talk to a man before you have a few drinks?
- Does alcohol remove your inhibitions to allow you to enjoy sex?
- Do you feel rejected and ashamed when you sleep with someone who doesn't call you afterward?
- Are you spending all of your money on alcohol?
- Do you have any medical issues, such as STDs?

Unlike the closet drinker, barhoppers are a social bunch who like to drink in groups. Also, with a group dynamic, there is usually someone in your posse who is drinking as much as you are. If you are drinking alone, as I did, you might realize that you have a problem, but if you are doing it with a friend, you can tell yourself that it's okay because you're not the only one. Group drinking doesn't happen only at a bar or a club. It can be any place women get together to bond and socialize, including the Junior League, charity functions, promotional parties, and women and wine events. The difference between the barhoppers and the binge drinkers is that the barhoppers aren't going out specifically to get drunk—they're going out for the camaraderie, to meet men, and to have a good time.

COCKTAIL CULTURE

If you were wondering just how deeply drinking is embedded in our society as a social ritual, the Museum of Art at the prestigious Rhode Island School of Design featured an exhibition in 2011 that looked at drinking and entertainment through the art of fashion and design. The exhibition included haute couture cocktail attire, from the little black dress to disco loungewear by iconic designers of the twentieth century: Pierre Cardin, Coco Chanel, Christian Dior, Halston, Jeanne Lanvin, Jean Patou, and Elsa Schiaparelli. It also displayed photography, advertising, and more than 150 decorative drinking objects, from an Art Deco cocktail shaker to a Tiki bar.

Again, social drinking is not the issue here; I'm talking about habitual drinking as a way to cover up the pain of your loneliness, discomfort, or feelings of desperation. The problem with drinking heavily when you are in your twenties or thirties is that you are in your prime childbearing years. The sexual encounters that you have when drunk might lead to STDs, pregnancy, rape, infertility, and emotional turmoil if the guy you slept with last night doesn't call. If you are a barhopper or you know someone who is, here are a few suggestions for what you can do:

- Make a pact to recover with your girlfriends. The same bonds that formed your friendship can be used with great success in the rehabilitation process.
- Volunteer at a soup kitchen. Barhoppers tend to be self-absorbed, so thinking of someone other than yourself can be spiritually and emotionally liberating. It will also introduce you to a new community, compared to people you might find at a bar.
- Join a gym so that you can work out with your friends. Having gym buddies is a lot healthier than having drinking buddies.
- Become a mentor. Check your local high schools to see whether they have a program for professionals who want to help teens get a leg up when they enter the workforce. Working with kids can be rewarding for both the mentor and the mentee.

Triggers for Barhoppers

The relapse triggers for barhoppers include failed relationships, unfulfilling jobs, and pressure to entertain clients. When you've graduated from college or left the safety of your parents' home after high school, you might find that the outside world is not always a friendly and accommodating place. You might also discover that drinking can make everything look and feel a whole lot better and can do wonders for the social pain of loneliness. For barhoppers, the pub crawl is how many single women in their twenties and thirties spend their Saturday nights, but this doesn't have to be the case anymore. Former barhoppers and friends can now find new ways to cope with their temptations, intimidations, and painful feelings of disappointment. Here are some ideas.

Looking for Romance

Nowadays, technology makes it unnecessary to search for a mate or a date at a bar. There are so many online dating services, such as Match.com, eHarmony, JDate, and ChristianSingles, that a companion is literally at your fingertips. You simply put "non-drinker" on your profile to weed out the male imbibers. There are even online dating services that cater to the sober community (see bullet list on page 54) if you want to cut to the chase without the chaser. Blogs that create an online community can be another way to socialize with like-minded people. Of course, you can't spend all of your time behind a screen, so you must eventually meet your online friend, which should always be a relatively short, simple outing in a public place, such as meeting for coffee or having lunch. If all goes well, you can meet for a dinner, but skip the premeal cocktail. If you are meeting a stranger you were introduced to online, make sure to let a friend know where you are going and call her when you get home. You could also check in by cell phone mid-date to let your buddy know that you are all right. The following are two specialized sites that cater to sober singles:

- **Soberandsingle.com** is an Internet website for people who are looking for love, dating, and romance in recovery, people whose common bond is their desire to date others who wish to be in an alcohol-free relationship. Dating can be daunting enough; now throw into the mix the fact that you don't want to go to a bar or a club to establish a relationship, and it's that much harder! Sober & Single claims to be completely dedicated to helping alcohol-free and drug-free singles find their special someone!

- **12stepmatch.com** is a recovery dating website where single sober women and men can bond and then meet for either sober dates or to become sober soul mates. This site works within whatever twelve-step program of recovery its members choose. Whether it's AA Singles, NA Singles, Al-Anon Singles, GA, OA, it claims to have thousands of members who are ready, willing, and un-enabled to embark on some sober meeting and greeting. You can search by country, state, city, or zip code and then narrow down your search further to your own twelve-step program. The site follows AA's recommendation that members wait a year before getting into a romantic relationship.

Real R&R

Another good way to avoid the awkwardness of dating in real life is to take part in some kind of activity where you and your date can both relax and have fun. Don't go to a movie or a play (at first) because you will spend two hours in the dark without speaking. Go to a ball game instead, but only if you truly like sports. Don't pretend to be who you're not (rigorous honesty, remember?), so choose an activity that fits your personality and one in which you can be yourself and fit in. Of course, there's a lot of drinking at sporting events, so don't do this if it is a trigger for you, and also avoid the tailgate parties. If you're a sports type who prefers being off the bleachers, take some swings in a batting cage or on a driving range. If you like adventure, go bungee jumping or take a balloon ride. Depending on where you live, you can go horseback riding, to a petting zoo, or to a museum if you're arty or intellectual. Visiting an amusement park is a great way to feel like a kid again, and screaming on a roller coaster is a fantastic tension reliever. There are so many activities to choose from that don't involve drinking. When you truly have fun without hiding behind the cloak of alcohol, you are better able to explore who you really are and can see with sharper eyes and a clearer head whom you would like to spend time with. It doesn't matter what you choose to do, as long as you feel comfortable doing it.

- **Throw your own sober soiree.** Next to public speaking, going to a party is one of the most anxiety-producing events for people, which is why "cocktail" usually comes before the word. We all have obligatory events we must attend, such as weddings, christenings, bar mitzvahs, and the like, so if you must go, order a club soda and lime so that you can mix and mingle with the drinking singles. No one will ask you what you're drinking, unless they offer you a refill. If you've just met someone, and you are not ready to come clean about being sober, just say you're allergic to alcohol. No one will blink a bleary eye. You can also throw your own sober party and invite the people you feel comfortable being with. You're on your own turf, so you will feel in control, and if you want to meet new people, ask each friend to bring someone you've never met. Having a friend introduce and vouch for someone else is a great social lubricant. Invite the group over for some Wii or Kinect games (men love this), and order in pizza if you hate to cook or you don't want to spend all of your time in the kitchen.
- **Group date.** Go group dating with your BFFs so that you can keep your girl posse close by while you socialize with new men. Your BFFs must be on the same page as far as the no-liquor policy goes, and you must tell the men beforehand that your itinerary doesn't involve bars or wine tastings.

5

Binge Drinking

"I tried to drown my sorrows, but the bastards learned how to swim."

—*Frida Kahlo, artist*

A large crowd has gathered at a local hotel, the self-proclaimed headquarters for spring break in Cancun. There is a buzz of youthful excitement in the air. It's the middle of a bright Mexican afternoon, and young people are swimming up to the pool bar for what is clearly not their first drink of the day. All await the main attraction, a bikini contest, which is the daily entertainment for those staying at this hotel.

Three visibly intoxicated girls are strutting onstage, their bikinis barely covering their tanned and toned figures. As hip-hop music pulses in the background, the emcee announces, "It's time to get wet, girls," over the sound system. Like a cop trying to control unruly protesters, he hoses the girls down, causing their bathing suits to cling even tighter. "Take it off!" he commands next, and, amazingly, they oblige, energized by the crescendo of hoots and whoops in the audience. "Show us some positions!" the ringmaster barks into the microphone, as if gorgeous naked girls are not enough to satisfy the Romans watching the sexual gladiators perform. The girls assume various sexual positions, including a simulation of oral sex.

Although one might think this is an isolated incident, similar scenes are being played out at countless spring-break destinations, sorority and frat houses, clubs, or anywhere that young people gather to engage in hormone-infused bacchanalias. Teen alcohol use is on the rise for the first time in a decade, a disturbing trend that could lead to long-term health risks, according to a 2010 survey released by the Partnership for a Drug-Free America. The study found that the number of high school students who said they drank alcohol in the last month rose 11 percent in 2009, with 39 percent of teens (or 6.5 million) reporting that they drink.

Even though some parents believe these antics are an inescapable teenage rite of passage, others are oblivious to what their high school or college-aged children are doing on their beach vacations or in their leisure time. In a survey of five hundred parents conducted by the American Medical Association, more than half of those polled were unaware that tour agencies market spring and grad breaks as a time for heavy drinking. Yet no matter how much faith and trust you have in your teenagers, peer pressure almost always trumps parental influence when it comes to drinking. Although I was never a binge drinker, I did experience a great deal of peer pressure to drink while I was in college. It was difficult to resist, and there were many times that I almost gave in to the pressure just to get my friends off my back.

When your child goes off to college or your high schooler goes to a party with friends, she might feel that she has a license to let loose without adult supervision. Yet many young people experience regret and depression when the party's over because, in the sober light of day, they are embarrassed by what they did the night before. Although they would like to exert their newfound independence, teenagers are still at an age where they desperately need boundaries and adult guidance. Giving your children too much freedom too soon can be like pulling the plug on a grenade.

It's a lesson that Lisa, a twenty-year-old college student, learned too late. Lisa woke up one morning after a dorm party to find that she had been beaten up. Worse than the black eye and the bruises she received was the fact that she had no memory of how she had gotten that way. "I knew that I needed to stop drinking," she told me later, "but this really scared me." Sometimes it takes a trauma such as this to scare a girl straight. For Melissa, not knowing where she was after a night of drinking and not being able to recall what happened was a wake-up call for help. Unlike boys, who might be amused by the aftermath of *Animal House* partying ("Dude, I didn't even know what town I was in!"), girls put themselves at risk of being raped, beaten, or even killed.

In Hanover, New Hampshire, police told a local news reporter that fraternity members at Dartmouth College cleared out a weekend house party before calling an ambulance for a nineteen-year-old woman who had passed out on a couch. The Sigma Alpha Epsilon fraternity at Dartmouth was the fourth Greek organization within a week to be charged with serving alcohol to minors, which is a felony.

For many young women, their first sexual experience occurs while they are under the influence. I've worked with countless teenagers throughout the years who confessed, "I never would have slept with him if I wasn't drunk." Would Natalee Holloway, the teen who disappeared in Aruba during her high school graduation trip, have gotten into a car with her alleged killer Joran van der Sloot had she not been drinking heavily that night? Tragically, we will never know the answer.

It also begs the question, why has there been an increase in the number of young women who binge drink these days? The desire to drink is certainly not new, but the driving forces behind most excessive drinking among young people are peer acceptance and pressure. One seventeen-year-old daughter of a friend admitted that she drank because that's what all of her friends did. She didn't particularly want to, she told me, but she couldn't stand the idea of not fitting in. Adolescents experience a torrent of emotions, including social anxiety and pain. "I don't know who I am yet. I want to be like everyone else. I'm not popular. I don't like myself. I hate my life. My parents don't understand me. My boyfriend rejected me." Whatever the issue, alcohol acts as both a pain reliever and a social lubricant during these turbulent years.

Alcohol is also a way for teenagers to establish their identities. In a culture that equates drinking with being hip, teens dread being labeled a nerd or a narc. Even at my age, people look at me and my husband askance when we go out to dinner and order iced tea instead of cocktails. They're afraid we might be boring. What they don't realize is that we love to have fun—we simply like to have it with clear heads! It's easy for us to laugh off these false judgments, but imagine what this kind of social alienation feels like to a teenager who cares deeply about what others think of her.

In addition, teens are a much sought after demographic for marketers of spirits. Take wine coolers, for example, which were created to appeal specifically to women. They are pink-colored and taste like a fizzy soft drink. Nowadays, one can pick up a six-pack of spiked lemonade at the nearest 7-Eleven for a sweet little buzz. As was the case with Virginia Slims, the long, lean cigarette that was targeted at women with the faux feminist jingle "You've come a long way, baby," purveyors of alcohol have found a female-friendly customer base that once almost exclusively belonged to men.

For the most part, girls who drink too much are not ashamed of their binge drinking, but they do feel guilty about what happens afterward. They might black out, get raped, or have a sexually explicit video of them go viral on the Internet. In some cases, as we know from numerous news stories, having embarrassing videos or pictures circulated online for the world to Google can be devastating, enough so to cause some girls at this vulnerable age to commit suicide. Teenagers do not have the ability to cope as well as adults do with their mistakes or bad choices. For them, being ridiculed or called names is the ultimate public humiliation. So they cycle back to the drinking to help them cope (or temporarily block) the shame that they feel, and alcohol becomes the way they deal with the pain.

The Teenage Brain

When it comes to good judgment, teenagers are arguably lacking. This is why shows such as *Jackass*, which feature clips of young men putting themselves in physically dangerous situations, or the female equivalent, the *Bad Girls Club*, which celebrates girls who behave badly, are so popular among young people. Videos of bullies attacking or humiliating another kid go viral on the Internet. Performing dumb and even life-threatening antics is not only a badge of honor, it's entertainment for those who would never dream of doing some of these things themselves. There is a voyeuristic pleasure involved in cheering these bullies and risk takers on. Bearing witness to bad or mean behavior makes you a part of the club.

There are biological consequences of binge drinking because the adolescent brain is not yet fully formed. When a young brain is exposed to alcohol, the chemicals can interrupt key processes of neural development and possibly lead to cognitive impairment. In one study of fifteen- and sixteen-year-olds, the alcohol-dependent group of teens had greater difficulty remembering words and simple geometric designs after a ten-minute interval than did those who were sober.

In addition, teenagers don't have the experience (or the good sense) to know when to stop drinking. They like the way alcohol makes them feel, and the more they drink, the greater the buzz and the less adolescent pain they feel. Given that alcohol is absorbed into the bloodstream in only five to ten minutes, and its effects last for several hours, depending on the amount ingested and how quickly it is consumed, it is easy to overindulge. For young women, who have less water in their bodies than young men do, alcohol is absorbed even faster into the bloodstream, which puts girls at an even greater risk, both physically and mentally, when they binge-drink.

My Entire Family Saw Me Win a Wet T-Shirt Contest on National TV

Following is one woman's story of how too much drinking one night led her to do something that she regretted for years afterward.

On the last night of our spring break vacation, a group of friends and I went on a popular Booze Cruise offered in Cancun. The cruise featured a short boat ride to a nearby island, followed by dinner, onstage drinking games, a wet T-shirt contest, and all the alcohol one could possibly want. As we boarded the boat, we learned that the *Wild on E!* crew was coming along and would be filming all of the evening's drunken debaucheries for a future episode.

Fueled by alcohol, the thought of being on TV, and the desire to make my last night in Cancun one to remember, I spontaneously entered the wet T-shirt contest without my friends' knowledge. I was known as the shy, quiet girl in the group, and I wanted to prove that I, too, could be wild and fun.

When the coordinators called for participants, I ran backstage to prepare for the contest, not knowing what to expect. Contestants flung their tops and bras on the ground, replacing them with thin white T-shirts supplied by the staff. A coordinator twisted the contestants' T-shirts into large knots that he tightened with his teeth, transforming the loose-fitting shirts into tight, midriff-bearing tops. I exchanged my black halter for one of the shirts and chatted with the other contestants. "I can't believe I'm doing this," giggled one. "My boyfriend's going to kill me," another tittered. As for me, I wondered whether my friends had noticed my absence and what they were going to think when they saw me onstage.

The contest passed in a drunken blur. Each girl danced and/or gyrated onstage after being sprayed with cold saltwater. The crowd cheered and hooted for their favorite contestants, with the emcee eliminating girls based on this response. I obediently pranced about when called onstage and flashed my boobs when the urge struck me. The *E!* producers passed us waivers between dance-offs, and everyone signed her name before dashing off to flash her chest one last time. As the crowd eliminated more and more girls from the competition, I realized that I might actually win the silly thing, and before I knew it, I'd done just that. The grand prize was supposed to be a bottle of tequila, which I never received.

The episode aired approximately two months later, and just about everyone I knew saw the show, including several family members. My mom and younger brother saw it while sitting at home one weekend. Some cousins also saw the episode and discussed it with my father at the annual family reunion. My brothers' friends made lecherous remarks in class. A male friend of mine saw an uncensored version of the show in Canada. Girls in my sorority saw it. Guys I didn't even know approached me on campus and at dance clubs, asking if I was that girl from *E!* At first, I enjoyed the attention, but I eventually grew sick of it, especially when I continued to hear comments months, even years, after the show initially aired. What had at first seemed like harmless fun now threatened to haunt me indefinitely.

As the years passed and I grew more mature and less desperate for attention, I began to wholeheartedly regret what I'd done. Though *E!* has more or less retired the episode, I have nightmares that it will resurface just long enough for my in-laws to see. Ladies, if you ever find yourself in a similar situation, run! What may seem fun and cute when you're twenty only seems desperate and slutty when you're twenty-seven.

Triggers Points for Binge Drinkers

Not surprisingly, the triggers (things that may cause an alcoholic to relapse) for binge drinkers are primarily peer related. Teenagers often find themselves in situations where friends encourage them to drink. Sex is another trigger for adolescents who are not yet comfortable with their bodies and with their sexuality. Alcohol eases the stress and the pressure that come with growing pains and the awkwardness of new relationships. Of all of the groups I've worked with, teenagers have the most difficultly coping with the transition from girlhood to womanhood.

So, how should teenagers deal with this often painful transitional period? Here are a few proven techniques teens can use to cope with their trigger points:

- **Avoid situations that make you uncomfortable.** If you go to a frat, sorority, or house party where there will be liquor, you are going to be hard-pressed to say, "Thanks, but no thanks." Girls at this age simply don't have the sense of self to resist peer pressure or their desire to have "fun." The only way to keep from drinking is to stay away from parties where there is booze and find other ways to have fun that don't involve drinking or taking drugs. Tell your friends that your folks won't let you go, that you have a test to study for, or that you've been grounded for life. Parents don't mind being the bad cops as long as it keeps their children out of the hospital or away from the real police.

- **Find your passion.** Replacing alcohol with a spiritual ideology is one of the most successful forms of recovery. That said, there are plenty of other activities to choose from that will give alcoholic girls a sense of community and a new-found feeling of achievement and self-esteem.

Theater groups; school or community shows (yes, Glee Club is now cool); environmental causes (recycling, wild-life and animal rescue, global warming issues); art classes; teen travel groups (not spring break–oriented, but ecotour-ism trips where teens help clean up the beaches destroyed by Hurricane Katrina or build houses, such as with Habitat for Humanity); bringing food to the elderly or the infirm through Meals on Wheels; tutoring younger kids, either through private lessons or through organizations such as Big Sister; joining sports teams such as soccer, volleyball, or basketball (there's nothing like winning a game to bolster one's self-esteem, but the real bonding comes with being accountable to your teammates and to a coach, which men and boys have experienced for centuries). Whatever sober activity you choose, isn't it better to make memories that last a lifetime (and that you can put on your résumé should you want to go to college or find a job) than not to remember what you did the night before?

- **Find alternative peer groups.** Although some young people go to and are helped by AA, others might not feel comfortable listening to the testimony of a sixty-five-year-old drunk who has been living in a shelter. This is why you should seek out teen-only AA meetings or an alternative recovery peer group. These meetings allow girls and young women to be with people their own age, who understand their issues and are willing to get in one another's face with streetwise advice and tough-love confrontation, if necessary. These groups, composed of peers struggling with similar problems, are great for helping girls deal with the pain of being an adolescent in transition.

- **Find online social networks that support the new, sober you.** Blogs create immediate feedback through an online community, while maintaining the kind of anonymity that one gets through AA. If someone sees a post from another person who is suffering, she can immediately send an e-mail, saying, "You sound really down today. Can I help?" Teenadviceblog.com is a place where teens and adolescents can get advice from their peers who are struggling with various issues, including drinking. There is also a blog for Teens of Alcoholic Parents (Helpteenswithap@ hotmail.com) for people who suffer from the effects of having an alcoholic parent, whether they are in recovery or not.

- **Get a mentor.** Family conflict is a major trigger point for many young girls. This is the period where there is often a great deal of family strife caused by a boyfriend whom the parents don't approve of, failing grades, or a clash of social values. Research shows that the single most important preventive factor for adolescents in crisis is having an adult other than a family member who is involved in your life so that you have someone to help you learn to cope with the pain of growing up in a healthy way. It could be a therapist, a coach, a youth director, a teacher, a neighbor, or the parent of a friend. It doesn't matter who it is, as long as that person cares about you and spends time with you and is able to walk you through the tough times.

Check your campus counseling center and sign up. If you are in high school, go to the guidance counselor, who will recommend someone you can talk to, free of charge or on a sliding scale. Keeping your pain bottled up inside will only make matters worse, and there is never any downside to speaking with a professional. You don't have to choose the first one you see, either. Visit a few to find someone whom you feel most comfortable talking to. Nothing gets accomplished when personalities clash.

- **Try getting high grades, instead of getting high.** Focusing on academics is another way to siphon off that energy you once put into scoring liquor and getting drunk. The rewards of succeeding in school can change your future forever, and scholarships that require you to maintain a certain grade point average can be wonderful motivators to make you stop partying and start studying.

  The good news is that it's never too late to learn, and I don't mean only calculus or philosophy. We teach basic life skills at my university's recovery center, such as how to handle money, how to interview for a job, how write a résumé, or how to shop and cook for yourself. It sounds ridiculously simple, I know, but these are the kinds of lessons everyone must learn. There is no shame in taking a course that will teach you the tricks of the trade to help you survive in a sober world.

- **Learn how to handle bullies.** Bullying has reached epidemic proportions in our middle and high schools and is a major cause of social pain. It used to be considered a rite of passage for growing up: deal with it, fight back, and don't tattle were some of the less helpful solutions given by adults back in the day. The first thing you must do is tell someone. This is not tattling—this is reporting. School administrators are now taking this problem seriously because they know that bullying can result in substance abuse, social isolation, depression, and even suicide.

Bullies are generally insecure people, but they tend to gather gangs around them who encourage their bad behavior. Do not engage the bully in a fight. Move yourself physically away from him or her. If you are being bullied online or by text messaging, change your number, e-mail address, or blog and alert your social network. Don't go online or use your cell phone until the problem stops.

If you are being ostracized because you're overweight, drinking will only make matters worse. I gained thirty pounds when I was drinking, and it came off as soon as I sobered up. The best way to cope with bullies is to find friends who support and love you no matter what you look like. At the same time, change your lifestyle by eating more nutritiously and exercising. Most young people who are overweight are emotional eaters. They eat when they are depressed, they eat when they are stressed, and they sometimes eat when they are happy. The same goes for drinking.

Try keeping a journal or a private blog (do not go on Facebook, where people can have access to your personal thoughts). Write about what you're feeling, not about what you're eating. For example, "I felt upset today because the popular girls called me names, so I sat in the corner of the cafeteria and ate a bag of Cheetos." It might be helpful to share your emotional journal with your mentor or join an Overeaters Anonymous group (www.oa.org).

What Can Parents Do?

Short of locking your teenagers in their room until they're twenty-one, the best-case scenario is to discourage your teenage daughters from drinking in the first place. Unfortunately, as a recent survey from the Partnership for a Drug-Free America and the MetLife Foundation revealed, one in five parents say they feel incapable of preventing their kids from trying drugs and alcohol. Yet don't let this scary statistic stop you from trying. There are several things you can do to either prevent or stop your teen from drinking.

One earmark of adolescence is the belief that you are inde-structible. In psychological terms, it is called the "personal fable," in which adolescents truly believe that "bad" things will never hap-pen to them. Parents need to have a conversation with their teen-agers about the real risks involved in excessive drinking. Remind them that in the United States, drinking under the age of twenty-one is against the law. Ask your daughter whether she is willing to risk the consequences if she gets caught, and let her know what those consequences are. Granted, for some teens this only makes the allure of alcohol even greater. Nevertheless, tell them what the penalties are in your state for driving under the influence. Explain what a criminal record will do to their chances of getting into col-lege or finding a job in the future, especially in these difficult eco-nomic times. Moreover, will they be able to live with themselves if they injure or kill someone in a drunk-driving accident?

If you suspect that your daughter has a drinking problem, ask her what's causing her pain. If she doesn't want to talk to you, get someone whom she trusts, whether it's a psychologist, a school counselor, a pastor, another parent, or even a peer. It doesn't mat-ter who it is—as long as the lines of communication are open, you will have a fighting chance to tame your daughter's normal ado-lescent tendencies, as well as her wild and compulsive behavior.

Remember, the need to fit in and to be accepted are strong motivating factors that often win out over parental influence. Ado-lescence can be a turbulent period of rebellion, where redefining roles and asserting independence lead to experimenting with alco-hol and drugs. If you still have a good relationship with your daughter, and she is confiding in you about peer pressure to drink, tell her it's time to find other friends who will like her for who she is. Explain that this is what *true* friendship is about. Here are some other things you can do:

- **Encourage her to find and pursue healthy areas of interest.** Let your teen have some choice about what she does, be it music, dancing, languages, sports, writing, environmental causes, or horseback riding, so she feels as if she has some control.

- **Unplug your daughter.** Facebook, texting, Wii, MySpace, iPhones, and iPads can be isolating and make it more difficult for parents to keep track of their teen's friends. Put time limits on screen time, or use it as a reward for completed homework, good grades, and chores well done.
- **Help your teen find a part-time job so that she isn't idle after school.** She can reward herself with some new clothes or a movie with the money she earns babysitting, as long as she saves some for future expenditures (such as college) and tithes a portion to a charity of her choice. This teaches children about fiscal responsibility, as well as generosity.

When parents ask me about how much privacy they should allow their teenagers, the answer is simple. Like it or not, it is your job as parent to monitor your children's lives. I can't tell you how many people tell me, "We know she's drinking with friends; we just pray that she's careful," to which I say, "You don't have to accept or condone this behavior!" Know who your children's friends are, and make sure you meet their parents. If her friend does not have the proper supervision or the same values as your family, explain to your daughter why she must put an end to the relationship. You might be the bad guy for a while, but trust me, it's worth it in the long run.

It's our job as parents to instill values, set boundaries, and make rules. It's okay to tell your daughter that if she comes home drunk again, she is grounded until she graduates. Write out a contract listing what she is expected to do and what she will get in return if she complies. Put the contract up on the refrigerator (see a sample on pages 70–71). Set high expectations for her behavior. If she does her chores and homework, she can go out on Saturdays with friends, as long as she is back by curfew. Whatever you do, be consistent. If the rule is broken, there must be consequences. It doesn't matter if she is five minutes or one minute late, say good-bye to the cell phone, the BlackBerry, or the iPad.

Remember, kids are afraid to say no to their friends, so it's okay for you to be the scapegoat. Your daughter can then say, "I'd love to go out with you guys, but ever since I got caught drinking, my parents give me a breathalyzer test when I get home." It may sound strange, but it works. You can even purchase an alcohol-level analyzer for well under $100 should you find it necessary to test your child. I believe that if children are living in your house, everything they own belongs to you. Don't be afraid to use their dependence on you to control their behavior. Sometimes these are life-or-death situations!

Former child actress Melissa Gilbert, now a mother of four and a recovering alcoholic, told to a reporter from the *ParentDish* blog about her philosophy on raising children. "I love my children to death, but as long as they're under my roof and they're under 18, they have no privacy," says Gilbert. "I have access to Facebook, to journals, to e-mails, to every way they communicate, including text messages, and I search regularly. I don't think that a child under 18 can handle privacy. Privacy is where the problems start. I grew up in the public eye, but I had a very private life and nobody knew what I was doing and I was going on three- or four-day binges."

Some parents might find this harsh, but there is a big difference between being authoritarian and being authoritative. You are their parent—not their pal. If you love your child, you owe it to her to make sure that she is safe. Why in the world wouldn't you do whatever you could to help her make good decisions? You must risk being disliked (temporarily) or playing bad cop, at least until she has earned back your trust, or she is no longer living under your roof.

If your daughter is twenty-one or older, and you suspect that she might have a drinking problem, ask her whether she has had experiences that cause her concern (hangovers, blackouts, car accidents, and so on). If you can't get her to stop drinking, encourage her to limit herself to no more than two drinks during the evening. Although this won't work with problem drinkers, it might stop your daughter from becoming one. In some cases, it might be necessary to get your daughter into a treatment center. Just let her know that you are there, if and when she needs you. Remember that she is probably experiencing some levels of pain in her life, and it is an opportunity for you to help before it is too late.

Think about it this way: these are your little girls. They *need* you to protect them and keep them safe. You wouldn't let them drive without first giving them driving lessons, and you wouldn't let them go sailing without life jackets. Why would you let your daughters drink alcohol or go to a bar without giving them the tools that can save their lives?

Behavior Contracts

Following is a sample of a behavior contract that you can use with an out-of-control teenager. Remember to clearly define the behaviors that you expect from her. "Rachel needs to be more respectful," is too vague, but "Rachel will not talk back, roll her eyes, curse, or yell at her parents or siblings" is not.

You can and should allow your teen to negotiate the rewards that will motivate her to change her behavior. If she wants to make her curfew later, that's unacceptable, but maybe she can get a bit more computer time or an item of clothing she's been coveting should she stick to the contract. The basic rule in choosing these "reinforcers" is that they should be motivating, inexpensive, and not time-consuming.

As for punishments, occasionally a penalty clause is necessary. If so, keep these consequences small and mild, such as taking away a privilege. The deal is, teens may negotiate the behavior and the rewards but not the contract itself, which is set in stone. If she breaks the rules, there must be consequences.

SAMPLE BEHAVIOR CONTRACT

Behavior expectations are:

1. _____

2. _____

Privileges for meeting the conditions of the contract:

1. _____

2. _____

Consequences/restrictions for failing to meet the conditions of the contract:

1. _____

2. _____

    I understand that I must meet all of the behavior expectations in order to earn all of my privileges each day. Failure to meet the behavior expectations will result in the consequences/ restrictions specified. Privileges and/or consequences will be earned on the same or the following day.

_____
Child's Signature

_____
Parent's Signature

For more information on prewritten behavior contracts, go to www.parentcoachplan.com. or www.teenbehaviorcontracts.com.

6

When Mothers Drink

In an early episode from the TV series *Mad Men*, set in the early sixties, advertising exec Don Draper is entertaining colleagues at his suburban home with his wife and family. His daughter, who looks to be around six or seven, is mixing and serving gin and tonics to guests as if she were a seasoned bartender. Although the Draper family may be fictitious, back in the day it was not uncommon for adults to throw cocktail parties while the children looked on or even helped serve the drinks. I remember many times when my parents had parties with friends where I was asked to help serve the drinks.

Flash forward to today, and you will find a retro-trend among mothers who are mixing libations and parenting. It seems that an increasing number of stressed-out moms are using cocktail play-dates and boozy birthday parties as a way to help ease the monotony of motherhood. Even in these health-conscious and child-centric times (the cigarettes are gone and the bike helmets are on), these momtini mothers want to have their birthday cake and drink, too.

Melissa Summers, the Michigan mother who is said to have coined the term "momtini," attracted so many readers when recounting her tales of serving Bloody Marys at children's play-groups on her Suburban Bliss blog, she began selling T-shirts, mugs and underwear emblazoned with her logo. And actress and author Christine Mellor argues in her tongue-in-cheeky book *The Three-Martini Playdate: A Practical Guide to Parenting*:

> Why not have an afternoon cocktail party? Sure, invite the kids. It's your child's birthday after all. If you plan on hav-ing more than a few children over to celebrate, hire a neigh-borhood teenager to keep an eye on the tykes while you and the other parents sip chilled alcoholic beverages. . . . Lemonade provides refreshment for those too young to appreciate distilled spirits, and the simple addition of a fine vodka creates an easily made and remarkably tasty bever-age for an exhausted and grateful grown-up.

Mellor even supplies readers with a martini recipe that "all young children should know how to make for their parents and other thirsty grown-ups who drop by around five o'clock." Although Melissa is not advocating mixology training before you potty-train your tot, she and a rapidly growing community of kin-dred spirits adamantly believe there is nothing wrong with drink-ing responsibly at play group gatherings. Blogs such as *Mommy-wantsvodka* are sprouting up on the Internet, and Babybites.com now sponsor happy hours in New York City around what used to be tea time (4 p.m.). Twittermoms.com hosts a monthly wine tast-ing where mothers indulge in an alcoholic treat and tweet.

"We take exception to the claim that social drinking in the presence of our children is a sign of irresponsible or bad parent-ing," reads the opening statement on the *Mothers for Social Drink-ing* blog. "Further, we contend that it is *moderation* that makes responsible drinkers, and that our society has more to fear from the poor judgment and intemperance of institutions which prey on parental insecurities." (Italics added.)

Similarly, an angry J. D. Griffioen, a contributor to the *Parent-Dish* blog, said the following after reading an article about the cocktail playdates in the *New York Times*:

Frankly, I'm sick of the whole mythology that once you have kids you have to become uptight about everything and buy a minivan and move to the suburbs and let all your values disintegrate into some hollow shell of how you saw your own parents. The whole point made by moms who drink during play dates is that alcohol is more of a symbol than anything else: they're not getting wasted, but the drink is a symbol that they haven't completely let go of who they are and let their kids overrun their lives entirely. . . . I say it's okay to drink around your kids. In fact, I'm going to go crack a Bells Double Cream Stout right now.

Yet others, such as Stephanie Wilder-Taylor, the mother of three young children and the author of the pro-momtini book *Nap Time Is the New Happy Hour*, worried that she had been drinking too much. She posted the following on her *Babyonbored* blog called "My Sobering Secret":

I drank often when Elby was a baby to help deal with the stress of a new infant. I found myself drinking more than I had before I became a parent and I drank with other moms to bond and unwind (yes, I'm the cocktail play-date mom and I stand by it being a healthy thing to do in moderation, in walking distance, (if you're not me). . . . For others it might be a once in awhile treat to go out and have a couple of cocktails. For me, it's become a nightly compulsion and I'm outing myself to you; all of you: I have a problem.

Stephanie, who's been sober since her public confession in May 2009, said that her harried married life led to her status as a champion of the cocktail mom, and she admitted that she is still a bit squeamish about her change of heart. "It's embarrassing to be all 'Rah, Rah Rah! Gooo BOOZE!' only to zip off with my tail between my legs, saying, 'Never mind, I've joined the other team,'" she wrote later. "But it's what I had to do."

Why are so many mothers today reaching for the wine bottle, along with the baby bottle? Research shows that better-educated women are more likely to drink excessively than less-educated ones are, as are women who work outside the home. For younger moms who are loath to give up their once vibrant social lives after having babies, cocktail playdates are a way to continue the party after motherhood.

New York magazine contributor Jennifer Senior described this frustration that some mothers feel in her article titled "Why Parents Hate Parenting." This is especially true, she noted, for women who have careers that are often more rewarding than a poke in the eye by a toddler's flying Lego.

> There was a day a few weeks ago when I found my 2½-year-old sitting on our building doorstep, waiting for me to come home. He spotted me as I was rounding the corner, and the scene that followed was one of inexplicable loveliness, right out of the movie I'd played to myself before actually having a child, with him popping out of his babysitter's arms and barreling down the street to greet me. This happy moment, though, was about to be cut short and in retrospect felt more like a tranquil lull in a slasher film. When I opened our apartment door, I discovered that my son had broken part of the wooden parking garage I'd spend about an hour assembling that morning. This wouldn't have been a problem per se, except that as I attempted to fix it, he grew impatient [and threw a Lego], narrowly missing my eye. I recited the rules of the house (no throwing, no hitting). He picked up another large wooden plank. I ducked. He reached for the screwdriver. The scene ended with a time-out in his crib.

> As I shuffled back to the living room, I thought of something a friend once said about the Children's Museum of Manhattan—"a nice place, but what it really needs is a bar"—and rued how, at that moment, the same thing could be said of my apartment. Two hundred and forty seconds earlier, I'd been in a state of pair-bonded bliss; now I was guided by nerves, trawling the cabinets for alcohol.

In addition, there's been a huge cultural shift in the way we parent. Before the rise of the modern feminist movement, our mothers and grandmothers seldom asked, "What about me?" They believed it was their duty to get married and have kids. Motherhood, with all of its mess and self-sacrifice, was their lot in life, and they made the best of it. Many believed, as my mother did, that children were a blessing, and they respected their role in life, knowing that it was one of the hardest and most important jobs in the world.

Of course, not everyone wore the badge of motherhood with such enthusiasm. Many moms felt bored and restless and suffered from the social pain of isolation. They volunteered or got jobs that were mostly low-level and female-friendly, while a nearby relative watched the kids. They also found ways to escape. They went to parties, played bridge with friends, and got babysitters or plunked the kids in front of the TV while they found other forms of entertainment.

Yet times have changed. What our foremothers understood, which is sometimes missing in the daily lives of moms today, is the separation of adult and kid time. It's not enough anymore to put three squares on the table and make sure that the kids leave the house clean and fully dressed. Today, women are expected to be mother, wife, housekeeper, cook, and, in more and more families, financial contributor or even breadwinner. Add to this, the recent phenomenon of the "helicopter mom" who acts as class parent, fund-raiser, enrichment seeker, social secretary, and role model.

Part of this hovering mothering trend is driven, in part, by the emotional pain of fear. Fear that someone will snatch your child off the street, making "Go outside and play" as quaint as the milkman. Fear of gum disease if we don't help our kids brush and floss. Fear of skin cancer if we don't slather them with SPF 50. Fear of fractures if they don't have knee, elbow, and shin guards when they go scooting. Fear that they will be poisoned by E. coli or insecticides if we don't buy organic. Fear that they will fall behind intellectually if we don't help with the homework, read to them every day, sign them up for music and language lessons, and cut back or cut out TV and Wii. Fear of obesity and social humiliation if they don't join the soccer team or Little League. And fear that they are involved in too many extracurricular activities so they are just as overextended and exhausted as we are.

So when mothers find that it is nearly impossible to do all of this without imploding, they are understandably in need of a little stress relief. In short, it's enough to drive you to drink. "Mothers are so hard on ourselves and so are others," observes Purvi Roe, a stay-at-home mother of an infant and a toddler. "Never before in history have we been more judged, expected to be so perfect, as well as our kids. It is hard. So allowing ourselves to have time to relax and not be perfect is very important because at the end of the day we are only human."

Jaymie, a forty-two-year-old New York mom, explained it this way: "I had gone through my twenties and most of my thirties as a free spirit with only myself and my husband to care about. So, once I had a child, it was difficult for me to give up some of my independence. I couldn't travel as much as I used to, and I couldn't go out drinking with my friends. My cocktail playdates allow me and my fellow moms a time to kick back and relax without the babysitter meter running at $15 an hour."

For those who enjoy sipping wine while their children play, let me just say that I do not believe that social drinking is a gateway to alcoholism. Sharing wine and conversation with the girls while a clown is bending balloons at a party can be downright therapeutic. As I said earlier, similar to indulging in the occasional ice cream sundae, there is nothing wrong with anything in moderation. Yet if you eat a lot of ice cream as a way to cope with a deeper problem, you are going to get fat. The same goes for alcohol. What is true for momtini mothers and just about every type of women drinker in this book is that there's a difference between social drinking and habitual drinking.

Whatever side of the fence you fall on, everyone agrees that putting the kids in the backseat and driving home after the proverbial one too many is the most frightening part of the cocktail playdate. National statistics from 2007 show that the number of women arrested for driving under the influence (DUI) has risen nearly 30 percent in the last decade. In 2009, a woman named Diane Schuler and her husband were at a lakefront campground in upstate New York with their two-year-old and three young nieces. Their summer outing ended tragically and made national headlines after she crashed into another car while driving the wrong way on a parkway. Eight people, including Diane and the children, died in the accident. According to the toxicology report, high levels of alcohol and marijuana were found in her system, and a shattered bottle of vodka was found by police under the seat of her minivan.

Fortunately for Elizabeth Dotsie of Maine, her wake-up call came before it was too late. She found herself reaching for the wine in order to finish making Halloween costumes for her four-, six-, and ten-year-old. "Later, I took them to a party at the local Catholic church after drinking all day," says Elizabeth, whose kids are now fully grown. "I stopped drinking after that."

Another, less obvious, risk occurs when alcohol dulls the senses that alert us to when our babies are crying or that allow us to use the eyes in back of our head when our toddler has just grabbed a steak knife off the kitchen table. By not drinking, we won't let our necessary guard down while our children are around. One mom, who wished to remain anonymous, reported passing out after a playdate where alcohol was served in her home, while her four-year-old slept inside and the babysitter, who was outside with her seven-year-old, repeatedly rang the doorbell. Imagine that same scenario without the babysitter, and you'll see what I mean.

It's wonderful to get together with other moms, and I encourage all mothers to be active outside the home to help them cope with the social pain they often feel. I also caution them against using alcohol as a rallying point. The get-together should be about the bonding, not about the drinking. I guarantee that if you get a group of women together who are drinking and another group who isn't, the women who are sober will feel more connected. Alcohol might make you feel more open and relaxed, but it won't help you connect in a genuine way. There are many healthier outlets for bonding with other mothers than getting together over drinks. Here are a few ideas:

- Hire a babysitter and go out to lunch or a movie or get a manicure/pedicure. Going to a park or a library to read a book is free and a great way to get some relaxing alone time that will stimulate your otherwise dormant brain cells.
- Pack up the kids and go on a group shopping trip. If you'd rather give than receive, enlist your kids in gathering up old but gently used toys and clothes and take a field trip to the Salvation Army.
- Volunteer for a charity (other than fund-raising for your kids' school) where you and other mothers are helping others in need.
- Go running, play tennis with a friend, or join a gym, especially one with child-care services. If you can't find or afford a sitter, join or start a Strollercize group (visit www.strollercize.com for more information) or take mommy and me yoga classes.
- Start a mommy blog. Blogs are a great way to vent your frustrations and bond with other like-minded mothers.
- Go to a museum or a gallery (for adults). Get the recorded guided tour, and tune out the rest of the world so that you can concentrate on the beauty in front of you.
- Start a book club that serves food and nonalcoholic beverages only.

There are so many interesting, healthy alternatives to choose from, so go online, look at your local paper, and start thinking outside the sandbox.

SIDEBAR: COCKTAIL PLAYDATE GUIDELINES

The bottom-line rules for going bottoms-up during playtime are:

- Never, ever get in the car after drinking, no matter how sober you feel.

- Don't drink with your kids around when there are no other designated caregivers to step in and pick up the slack should you get too tipsy.
- If you must nip during nursing time, keep it to one small glass only.
- Make sure there is plenty of food to eat and water to drink.
- If you think you are drinking to cover up a bigger problem or some measure of pain in your life, or you are counting the days or the hours until you next uncork, you have a problem that needs tending to, and not with a bar in front of it.

If you want to kick your nappy hour habit, you must find new outlets that will help you cope with the drudgery of child care. Unlike going to an office or an outside job, where you can leave your work behind, being a mother is full time, especially if you count the hours that you worry while you are not with your children.

If you're a momtini mother, you need to understand that you are not a bad mother or crazy for not feeling happy with the way your life is at the moment. There is no such thing as being a perfect mother or having a perfect family or, for that matter, a perfect world. Much of my drinking was wrapped up in an illusion of "perfection" that simply does not exist! If you screamed at your kids today, don't beat yourself up about it. Give the kids a hug, and let them know that you're sorry you lost it. Good mothers are taught to put their kids and husband first, but you are no good to anyone unless you save yourself first. Think about what the flight attendant says when instructing passengers about what to do in case of an emergency. When the oxygen masks drop, you must put *your* mask on before the children's. How can you save your kids if you have passed out, unconscious? The same goes for being passed-out drunk.

This being the case, here are some sanity-saving suggestions for carving out some relaxing, worry-free mommy time:

- **Have a girls' night out**. First and foremost, disabuse yourself of the idea that drinking is the only way to kick back and have fun with your friends and that you've thrown your social life down the diaper genie once you've given birth. Organize a regular girls' night out (dinner, watching chick flicks, or dancing your boozeless booty off).

- **R&R versus the three Rs**. Moms need to find a place where they can take care of themselves, relax, and breathe poop-free air. Try going to a yoga retreat, doing meditation (see page 163 on the relaxation response), or take a simple soaking in a hot tub with the lights low, scented candles, and some bubble bath. Organize a self-help day with your friends, where you all meet for a mani-pedi, then have a spa lunch, followed by smoothies.

- **Avoid mommy brain**. If it's excitement and intellectual stimulation you're craving (and who doesn't need to spoon-feed her cranium while watching *Yo Gabba Gabba?*), consider going back to work when your kids are old enough and when you're ready. You can also get a work-at-home gig that will exercise your entrepreneurial muscles. Another good way to avoid mommy brain is to take continuing education courses in subjects that interest you, whether it's cooking, comparative religions, philosophy, or languages. Keeping your mind active will help ward off the baby blues and alleviate the mental pain of depression.

- **Exercise your body or your plastic**. Instead of meeting at 4 p.m. in the playground, meet your friends at the gym for a smoothie. If the gym offers child care, work out together so that you will feel better both physically and mentally. Can't afford a gym? Get a running stroller and start jogging. If exercise isn't your thing (and it should be, because it helps relieve stress and emotional pain and also burns that baby fat), try some modest retail therapy or window shopping.

- **Volunteer**. I know it's a cliché—the stay-at-home mothers who funnel all of their latent managerial energy into the PTA or PETA or PACs, but volunteering is one of the best ways to stay active and boost your self-esteem into the stratosphere. Raising $50,000 for your children's school at the annual auction or spring fair pays for a lot of books, supplies, and assistant teachers and is especially important when our educational system is also in recovery.

- **Blog, blog, blog.** Sometimes it's hard to get out of the house or the apartment for an AA meeting, so a great way to reach out to other mothers in recovery from the comfort of your own laptop is to blog about your feelings and day-to-day struggles. It's a way to make new friends and develop a wider support group of people who understand what you're going through and who will read and respond to your gripes about baby wipes. To wit, the following is a list of some of the funniest, smartest, and best mommy blogs chosen by Babble.com, which my coauthor, Jodie, who is also a mom, checked out for her daughter. Who knows? You might find the support you need during that hour or two of screen time while the kids are napping.

> *The Mommy Blog* (http://themommyblog.net): Writer, graphic designer, and divorced mother of three Melinda Roberts describes her blog as "Adventures from the Wonderbelly of Motherhood." Roberts writes witty observations and confessions about life in the trenches from the perspective of a Silicon Valley wonder woman.
>
> *Motherlode* (http://parenting.blogs.nytimes.com): *New York Times* columnist Lisa Belkin writes this "adventures in parenting" blog for smart, book-loving mothers. She quotes heavily from other mommy blogs, including the following survey on coping from across the pond: "In a survey of 5,000 British mothers by the Web site Net-mums.com, a high percentage of moms admitted they have not been entirely honest when discussing parenting issues with their parents. They fudged about 'coping in general' (69 percent) and 'coping financially' (46 percent) and 'time playing with children' (20.6 percent) and 'time kids spend watching TV' (23 percent) and 'food you feed your kids' (17 percent) and 'your sex life' (13.6 percent.)."

Finslippy (www.finslippy.com): A blog by a professional writer named Alice Bradley, whose tagline includes "wading in the shallow end since 2004" and who also writes parenting articles for women's magazines. Her blog has sections on "Let's panic about babies," "Mom-versations," and "Sleep is for the weak."

Free Range Kids **(how to raise safe, self-reliant kids without going nuts with worry)** (http://freerangekids.wordpress.com): Lenore Skenazy got a lot of flack for her book about giving kids more freedom to be independent, like back in the good old days when children could walk unescorted to school without fear of being snatched by a fanatic fringe cult member. This blog might not be good for mothers who are already laissez-faire parents due to their drinking, but it could give some helicopter moms permission to ease up on the hovering mothering.

Dooce (www.dooce.com): Heather Armstrong writes, in her words, about "poop, boobs, her dog, and her daughter." *Dooced* means to lose one's job because of one's website, which I assume is what happened to Heather. Here's a sample of one of her rants: "Have you ever been a stay-at-home parent? Do you have any idea the amount of rigorous work and emotion it requires? The tireless hours of performing tasks that will never earn you a raise or a gold star or *even be acknowledged by another human being?*"

Parent Hacks (www.parenthacks.com): Not-at-all hackish parenting tips from the real experts—moms—which include advice on homemade detanglers for stress- and tear-free hair brushing and better uses for a preliterate baby bookshelf, as shared below.

Meredith . . . shared her one-hack-led-to-another epiphany about the usefulness of bookshelves as toy storage: "I'm a new mom and was a little naive about when babies actually start to enjoy reading. I had neatly arranged my 9 month-old daughter's books on her bookshelf, but all she did was toss them around and chew the edges. . . . I picked some toys and displayed them on the shelf and now she loves to spend time choosing a toy. She is much more engrossed in her play than when I stuffed every-thing in a toy box."

Playgroups Are Not for Children (www.playgroup-sarenoplaceforchildren.com): Jennifer Doyle is a self-styled writer, photographer, foodie, mother, wife, SUV-driving Southerner-by-proxy. She started her blog to help herself deal with the monotony of days spent in her house in the middle of nowhere while her baby napped. Her bio says it all: "I'm Jennifer, mom to Carson, 5, and Ella, 3, wife and bossaholic to my husband Tate. I can eat my weight in nachos. On a related note, I wear Spanx."

Mom 101 (www.mom-101.com): The tagline for Liz Gumbinner's blog is "I don't know what I'm doing either." Who can't relate to that sentiment? She discusses how we can sometimes be "sanctimommies" who judge one another's mothering skills from the sidelines, and she includes subjects such as how to talk to your kids about tragedy (Answer: "No freakin clue") and things you never say to a stay-at-home mom: "Recently, I was chatting with a neighborhood mom, and when I innocently asked whether she still worked, she responded, a little snippy, 'Yes, every day. As all moms do.'"

7

Drunkorexia

D runkorexia, though not a recognized medical term, is a combination of alcoholism and eating disorders. The idea behind this syndrome is that women starve themselves during the day so that they can save the calories for a night of drinking. Several studies have found a rise in these dual disorders during the last decade, including one published in the journal *Biological Psychiatry* that revealed that about 25 to 33 percent of bulimics (purgers) also struggle with alcohol or drugs, and between 20 and 25 percent of anorexics have substance-abuse problems.

What makes this a potentially lethal cocktail of addictions is that the less food you have in your stomach, the faster the alcohol will race into your bloodstream. If you eat while you drink, however, food will absorb some of the alcohol. Doctors who treat drunkorexia say that getting women to kick alcohol is much easier than treating the eating disorder because you can live without booze, but you can't live without food. Serious anorexics see food as the enemy, while recovering alcoholics eventually learn to view liquor as a demon to be reckoned with.

Savannah, twenty-two, became a drunkorexic while she was a student at the University of Texas. She would stop eating during the day when she knew that she was planning to party that night. "I've always watched my weight and skipped meals to account for the high calorie count of alcohol," Savannah told a campus reporter for ABCnews.com. "It was just something I always did while in college as a normal part of my diet so that I could stay skinny but still go out and drink."

Savannah, who currently lives in Houston, says that she and her friends would swap ideas for skipping meals, which included working out instead of eating, having one tiny meal during the day, or, for the bulimics in the group, purging before going out. Despite knowing that what they were doing was foolish, at best, the desire to be thin and have "fun" was so strong that it became part of Savannah's weekend ritual. She said that seeing other women she knew drink heavily without gaining weight was another incentive.

At her mother's urging, the disturbingly thin Savannah attended counseling sessions for anorexia at college, but the therapy did nothing to change her behavior, even after graduation. "I've done [drunkorexia] for years, and I'm still healthy," she claimed. "And I'm skinny. That's the best of both worlds to me, so it's not likely that I'll stop doing it any time soon."

Women as Marketing Targets

Along with the traditional fashion, cosmetic, and other female-friendly pop-up ads that young women are bombarded with on Facebook or Google, they are targets for marketers promoting weight-loss tips and products. Men are not. In addition, blogs that promote being superskinny have been popping up on the Internet during the last few years, and books such as *Skinny Bitch* fly off the shelves. The pro-skinny credo recommends strategies for staying "model slim," including the "five-bite diet," in which one is instructed to take only five bites of food at each meal. Some sites also share techniques for drinking and not gaining weight.

For many in the throes of drunkorexia, staying thin becomes a badge of honor. Famous women often get publicly derided when they plump up, which only adds to the cultural obsession with weight (think Oprah pulling a wagon full of fat, Jessica Simpson in "mom jeans," and postbaby, postdivorce Christine Aguilera). Type-A women, who are competitive by nature, are susceptible to eating disorders, but rather than striving for the highest grades, a different bar has been raised (pun intended) for those who can drink the most and eat the least. Counting calories is the female version of Fantasy Baseball, a communal activity, but with very real and extremely dangerous consequences.

HOLLYWOOD'S DRUNKOREXIA

Lainey, the hilarious gossip hound and Canadian entertainment blogger, weighed in on the subject of drunkorexia after noticing the skeletal remains of several Hollywood actresses. Here's what she had to say. Ironically, an ad for SlimFast popped up when I was reading her cautionary Lainey.com entry.

Drunkorexia

I can't take credit for coining the term. That distinction belongs to dear divine Dean at eTalk with whom I was just discussing the phenomenon a few days ago.

Alright girls and gays . . . don't lie. I know you know what I'm talking about. It's not right and it's certainly not ok, but we've all done it at one time or another in our 20s so it's pointless to deny and I won't believe you if you do.

Let's say you have a wedding to go to. Or a party. And you must look fabulous. It's next Friday, you have an ensemble planned out, you will squeeze into it, you will bust your ass on the treadmill every day until you can barely stand, you will look like a piece of heaven, and that dirty, dirty bitch who cut her eye at you last time will slink back into the hole she came out of because she will realize she is no match for your superior hotness.

In order to ensure success, you will graze on vegetables and hummus for an entire week, and on the day of anticipated event, you will put nothing in your mouth, unless of course you are close to passing out, at which point a small, 2 cm x 2 cm piece of cheese is more than enough to put the fainting spell at bay.

So mission accomplished, you get to the par-tay, everyone loses their sh*t over your goddess-given gorgessity, you celebrate with a martini, and pretty soon that martini becomes three and all of sudden . . . where's the hunger? There ain't no hunger! You toast yourself all night long and when you wake up in the morning, your concave stomach fuels the Drunkorexia and you do it all over again on Saturday until Sunday comes around and you finally binge on eggs benedict and wash it down with popcorn in the afternoon followed by Taco Bell for dinner before heading back to work on Monday.

Sound familiar?

That, my friends, is Drunkorexia. Yes, yes. It is sooooo wrong. It is awful and f*cked up and disgusting and I know. But it is also an example of the awful and f*cked up and disgusting things women do to themselves for one night of glory before returning to sanity 24 hours later. And that is my point. Most of us return to sanity. Most of us go back to eating and slaving away at the gym from Monday to Friday, most of us are flawed and human but also practical and SMART. Drunkorexia for us is but a temporary lapse in judgment.

Drunkorexia's Roots in Addiction

Whether it's a girl-bonding challenge or an obsession with appearance that's fueling the drunkorexia, at its root, it is still an addiction. According to the National Institute of Alcohol Abuse and Alcoholism, alcoholism and eating disorders are frequently accompanied by other psychiatric and personality disorders. It is crucial, therefore, that those suffering from this disorder seek treatment for each individual addiction separately in order for a cure to be effective.

Because drinking can be a way to alleviate social anxiety, and anorexia often stems from a desire to exert control over one's life, drunkorexics must learn better ways of connecting with people and develop a stronger and more positive body image. This could take years of therapy to accomplish, but it could also save your life, so it's worth putting in the time with professionals who have been trained to treat these problems separately.

For those who do not yet have a drinking problem but are tempted to skip and nip, there is new scientific evidence that will

hopefully encourage you to cut back on your alcohol consumption. A surprising new thirteen-year study of 19,220 American
women by JoAnn E. Manson, M.D., of Harvard Medical School
and Brigham and Women's Hospital found that compared with
nondrinkers, women who drank alcohol in moderation were actually *less* likely to gain weight and were at lower risk of becoming
obese. Does this mean that women should drink more as a form
of weight control? Of course not. Previous studies of men have
shown the opposite to be true. The reason for this discrepancy, Dr.
Manson explains, is

- Although male drinkers tend to add alcohol to their daily
  calorie intake, females tend to substitute alcohol for food
  without increasing the total calories.
- Due to metabolic differences, women break down the calories in alcohol faster than men do.
- Alcohol may rev up women's metabolism more than it does
  men's.

For these reasons and other obvious health concerns, the lesson
here, once again, is moderation. For normal-weight women who
already drink, light-to-moderate drinking may provide a modest
weight-control benefit. Yet keep in mind that even one drink per day
(5 ounces of wine, 12 ounces of beer, or 1.5 ounces of liquor) can
boost your cancer risk, so limit yourself to one drink no more than
three or four times per week or, alternatively, to half a drink per day.

Liquids Are Easier to Purge

Judy, now thirty-eight, became anorexic when she was twenty-
four. The New Jersey resident told the *New York Times* that she
starved herself for two months, taking only small bites of low-
calorie food as nourishment. Later she began bingeing and purging, throwing up entire boxes of cereal, whole pizzas, and fast
food, a disgusting habit that often cost her $80 a day.

She went in and out of treatment for several years in the late
1990s, but instead of getting better, she added another addiction

to her bulimia and began drinking in 2001. Judy would purge if she allowed herself to eat while drinking but would continue to drink more so that she could stay drunk. Like Judy, many bulimics use alcohol to help them vomit because liquid is easier to purge, not to mention the nausea they often experience when drinking on an empty stomach.

"In the beginning of my eating disorder I wouldn't touch alcohol because it is so high in calories," recalled Judy, who said she was hospitalized regularly for dehydration. "But I have the disease of *more*: I just want *more*, no matter what it is."

After two years of drinking, Judy joined a twelve-step program and checked herself into six residential rehab programs. Because she was uninsured, her treatment cost $25,000 and ultimately failed because it did not address her eating disorders, which continued unabated. Although Judy has been sober for more than three years, she is still struggling with bulimia. When she became pregnant, support groups helped her make progress with her eating disorder, but after having the baby, Judy said the temptation to binge and purge returned. "I had an excuse to eat," she said of her pregnancy. "I didn't care, and I loved it."

Alcohol—a Weighty Issue

Everyone from the Food and Drug Administration to tobacco manufacturers knows that smoking cigarettes can lead to cancer. It even says so on the package. Yet nicotine is addictive, so emphysema and lung cancer be damned—forty-six million people, nearly 20 percent of whom are in high school, continue to smoke. Alcohol can be equally hazardous to your health if abused. If you are a hard-core drinker, experts now know that showing you a picture of a diseased liver or even children mangled in a drunk-driving car crash might not be enough to get you to stop. Likewise, if you are a drunkorexic, I realize that showing you pictures of women with their ribs and other bones protruding won't get you to bite into that chicken fajita. I get it—you *want* to stop drinking and you want to start eating regularly, you know what you are doing is bad for you, but you just can't (or aren't motivated to, at least right now). You're addicted. With this in mind, I am going to appeal to another, sometimes stronger force in the female psyche—your vanity—which is why you are starving yourself in the first place. If I can't get you to stop abusing your body for health reasons, I will tell you how drinking affects the way you look. To start, take a realistic look at yourself in the mirror (which, I know, is difficult for anorexics to do). Even if you think your ninety-five-pound body is fat, women who drink heavily tend to neglect other parts of their appearance the way a sick cat does. They stop grooming themselves; they let their hair go; they dress in loose, sloppy clothes; and they even skip showering. Not a pretty picture.

When I was drinking, I gained thirty pounds, and, although I never stopped eating, I certainly didn't have a well-balanced, nutritious diet. There is still no doubt that heavy drinking can result in weight gain because alcohol contains empty calories, especially cocktails that have sugary mixers, such as fruit juice, soda, and syrups. The best way to stay at your optimal weight is not to skip meals but to skip the cocktails!

Check out this alcohol calorie breakdown if you want to know what you are pouring into your body, and perhaps it will encourage you to cut back or switch to alcohol-free beverages:

Red wine: A 5-ounce glass of wine is about 120 calories. A favorite among many women, red wine is touted for its heart-healthy antioxidant properties, but the sulfites in this wine can also trigger migraines and make existing irritable bowel syndrome (IBS) and type 2 diabetes worse.

White wine: Thought to be a bit lighter than red wine, a 5-ounce glass of white has about 120 calories, the same as red. Heavy intake of white wine, as with other alcoholic beverages, can cause you to gain weight, increase your triglycerides, and wake you up during the night.

Beer: A 12-ounce glass of regular beer has 150 to 200 calories per serving, so do math if you are downing a six-pack. They don't call it a "beer belly" for nothing. Even a light beer has

100 calories per serving, which is better but still not great if you're having more than one.

Brandy: Brandy is an aperitif that is produced by distilling wine. It is generally consumed straight and, like other alcoholic drinks, can increase your triglycerides and interfere with your sleep cycle. If you have type 2 diabetes, it can make your condition worse. A 1.5-ounce shot of brandy has about 100 calories, and nonalcoholic women shouldn't have more than one a day.

Rum, tequila, gin: These hard liquors are often combined with sugary beverages to make popular drinks such as margaritas, gin and tonics, piña coladas, and rum and cokes. A 1.5-ounce serving of these liquors contains about 100 calories, but when you combine it with other sugary beverages, you can really pack on the pounds.

Vermouth: Vermouth is typically not served on its own and is most often used as an ingredient in mixed drinks, such as martinis, and contributes 30 to 50 calories per ounce. Vermouth-containing cocktails can make you put on the pounds, increase your triglycerides, and interfere with your sleep. It is advisable to avoid vermouth if you have type 2 diabetes, gout, or irritable bowel syndrome.

Vodka: A 1.5-ounce shot of vodka (about 100 calories) is considered one drink. Vodka is another favorite among alcoholic women, because it is clear, can be easily hidden in other containers, and is often mistaken for water. Although some people like it straight, it is often combined with high-calorie, sugary mixers such as soda and fruit juice. Either way, vodka drinks can cause you to gain weight, increase your triglycerides, and interfere with your sleep.

Whiskey: A 1.5-ounce shot of whiskey (about 100 calories) is considered one drink. Sometimes thought of as a man's drink, whiskey is a hard alcohol that is distilled from fermented grains. It is commonly consumed straight up or on ice but may also be mixed with other drinks. Whiskey combined with soda and other high-calorie, sugary mixers can increase your triglyc-erides and interfere with your sleep cycles.

Do You Have an Eating Disorder?

According to the National Eating Disorders Association (NEDA), you know you have a problem if your attitude toward food, weight, and body size has led to rigid eating and exercise habits that are jeopardizing your health, happiness, and safety. Eating disorders may begin as a way to lose a few pounds or get in shape, but these behaviors can quickly spin out of control and become obsessions. Even if you don't have a full-blown eating disorder, you are miss-ing out on living if you spend all of your time dieting (and drinking).

Ask yourself (or someone you know) the following questions:

- Do you constantly calculate the number of fat grams and calories?
- Do you weigh yourself often and find yourself obsessed with the number on the scale?
- Do you exercise to burn off calories and not for health and enjoyment?
- Do you ever feel out of control when you are eating?
- Do your eating patterns include extreme dieting, prefer-ences for certain foods, withdrawn or ritualized behavior at mealtime, or secretive bingeing?
- Has weight loss, dieting, and/or control of food become one of your major concerns?
- Do you feel ashamed, disgusted, or guilty after eating?
- Do you constantly worry about the weight, shape, or size of your body?
- Do you feel as if your identity and value are based on how you look or how much you weigh?

If you answered yes to any of these questions, you could be deal-ing with disordered eating. These attitudes and behaviors can take a toll on your mental, emotional, and physical well-being. It is important that you start to talk about your eating habits and concerns now, rather than wait until your situation becomes more serious.

Tell a friend, a teacher, a parent, a coach, a youth group leader, a doctor, a counselor, or a nutritionist what you're going through. If this seems too scary or too difficult, you may want to start by going to www.NationalEatingDisorders.org or calling 800-931-2237 for more information and referrals. Someone from NEDA can help you plan what to say the first time you talk to someone about your eating issues. It is important to get some support to change the thoughts and behaviors you are experiencing now. If you are already in or seeking treatment for alcoholism, you need to find a specialist in eating disorders as well. Sober and bulimic is still no way to live!

The More I Drink, the More I'm into My Eating Disorder

Trish, a twenty-seven-year-old nurse, who has had an eating disorder for the last ten years, recently checked into her fifth treatment center or hospital. Like Judy, Trish struggled with anorexia before discovering alcohol. Before she was admitted, she reported having excruciating stomach pains and blackouts from lack of food.

Trish would starve herself during her eight- or twelve-hour shifts, staring at the clock while waiting for the time when she could have her first drink. Drinking, she said, relaxed her when she had to eat in front of other people, a huge source of stress.

"The alcohol is probably what kept any weight on me," she said in an interview with the *New York Times* before she started eight weeks of treatment. "Drinking helped me be less anxious," she said. "It helped me be more of Trish. The two go together: If I drink more, I'm more into my eating disorder and vice versa." After her second round of residential treatment, Trish said she was determined to stop her obsessions with food and alcohol. "I will not live my life like this," she said. "I've learned this time not to be ashamed and to love and forgive myself."

Support for Drunkorexics

Although some alcoholics are able to quit cold turkey, Drunkorexics must get structured therapy and the support of people who understand eating disorders. As mentioned earlier, organizations such as NEDA will help you or a loved one find a treatment center nearby. One center that addresses both eating disorders and addiction is the Remuda Ranch, which has facilities in Arizona and Virginia (www.remudaranch.com; 888-688-0472).

The Parent, Family & Friends Network (pffnetwork@myneda. org) is made up of nonprofessionals who offer loving support for those who suffer from this debilitating problem. NEDA Navigators, as they are called, are trained to help Drunkorexics build a support group of peers, as well as find professional help. There's also a group called Recovery Connection that can help you locate a treatment center in your area. Call its twenty-four-hour hotline, 800-993-3869, for assistance.

The webinar on the site aired on PBS as well and features a panel of experts who discuss what recovery from an eating disorder looks and feels like. The panelists include people currently in recovery and physicians who work with these issues. Because this disorder is so underreported, the most essential key to combating drunkorexia is bringing the issue out into the open on campuses and in other forums, such as group therapy. First, you must develop healthier eating habits and enough self-esteem to be comfortable with the way you look. Until you master the skills you need to recover from your eating and drinking problem, don't go out drinking on an empty stomach. Force yourself to eat something, even if it's pretzels or peanuts at the bar, and remember to drink lots of water, which will help dilute the alcohol.

8

When Bad Things Happen To Drunk Women

"[Drinking] is like gambling. You go out for a night of
drinking and you don't know where you're going to end up
the next day. It could work out good or it could be
disastrous. It's like the throw of the dice."
—*Jim Morrison, who died at twenty-seven*

The universal truth about alcoholics, whatever gender, is that they drink to feel *normal*. As I began to drink more and more, my tolerance for alcohol got to the point where I was drinking not to get drunk but to feel what had become my normal. After a time, alcoholics no longer seek the euphoria they experienced when they first started drinking. They simply drink to get through another day at work, to ease their anxiety, to forget their depression, or to dull their pain. The amount they drink is usually in direct proportion to the amount of pain they feel. Although some manage to stay afloat for a while, drowning one's pain and sorrow in alcohol typically will eventually produce myriad negative consequences, as described in the following sections.

Physical Consequences

While there are fewer female alcoholics than men overall, more women are adversely affected by drinking than their male counterparts are. An estimated five million women in the United States drink in a way that threatens their health and safety, according to the National Institute on Alcohol Abuse and Alcoholism (NIAAA). The NIAAA also found that female alcoholics are more prone than men to developing liver disease and heart and brain damage and are twice as likely to die from alcohol-related causes, such as suicide, accidents, and other illnesses.

Why the gender gap? Alcohol, unlike food, avoids the normal digestive process and heads directly to the bloodstream and into the water in our bodies. Because muscle tissue contains more water than fat tissue does, men, who have more muscle and less fat on average than women, have about 10 percent more water in their bodies. In other words, if a lean man and a lean woman of equal weight consume the same amount of liquor, the woman is still more adversely affected by alcohol because her organs will be exposed to more alcohol before it is broken down.

These biological differences play a role in both the short- and long-term effects of alcohol on women. Once alcohol enters the bloodstream, every organ, including the liver, the heart, and the brain, will be negatively affected. If you are a blackout drinker, the brain drain will be even worse. And if you think you are different because you can "hold your liquor"—think again. Research shows that those who are able to drink large amounts of alcohol in one sitting without getting sloppy drunk are at a higher, not lower, risk of developing an addiction. This is why a woman should never challenge a man to a chugging contest or try to drink him "under the table." Chances are, the table she will end up on is a gurney on her way to the emergency room.

Of course, no one takes that first drink intending to become an alcoholic. I certainly didn't, but developing a high tolerance for liquor is one way to get there. Here's the usual trajectory: You've had a long, stressful day, so you pour yourself a glass of wine or beer to take the edge off. The next time you feel stressed, you remember how much better you felt after that drink, so you have another stress-relieving nip. The problem with this cause and effect is that your body will need more and more liquor to get the same pleasurable feeling. This is what's called "tissue tolerance." Tissue tolerance happens with drugs, as well as with alcohol, and one can also build up resistance to over-the-counter medications, such as sleep aids and allergy medicine or prescription painkillers, such as Vicodin. Our bodies' tissue tolerance is what sets the wheels of alcoholism in motion. The more we are exposed to a substance, the more of it our bodies will need so that it can work its magic. Suffice it to say that alcohol abuse is a form of physical abuse to the body. So, if you want to live a long and healthy life, stop before you or someone else has to call 911.

Women who drink too much are at risk of developing the following health-related problems.

- **Heart disease**: Once thought to strike mostly men, heart disease is the leading killer of women in the United States. Among heavy drinkers, women are more susceptible to alcohol-related heart disease, even though women drink less alcohol during a lifetime than men do.
- **Car accidents**: It doesn't take much alcohol to impair our ability to drive safely. Research has shown that the chances of being killed in a car crash are higher after a 140-pound woman has one drink on an empty stomach. Although men make up the majority of drunk drivers in the United States, more young women are getting into drunk-driving accidents than ever before, according to a recent study published in *Injury Prevention*. According to researchers, this increase in risky behavior is caused by younger women's increasing desire to fit in.
- **Medication interactions**: There are more than 150 medications that should not be taken with alcohol. Drinking alcohol with any medication that causes drowsiness, such as antianxiety medications, antidepressants, and many cough

and cold medications, can increase a drug's sedative efforts. When taking any medication, it's important to read package labels and warnings carefully.

- **Breast cancer**: Many experts define moderate drinking for women as no more than one serving of alcohol (1.5 ounces of liquor, 4 ounces of wine, or 12 ounces of beer) a day. According to a new study published in the *Journal of Clinical Oncology*, however, even that moderate level of drinking may be too much for breast cancer survivors.

  Researchers followed 1,897 early-stage breast cancer patients for an average of 7.4 years, tracking cancer recurrences and deaths. Those who consumed at least three to four drinks per week (an average of roughly one-half drink per day or more) were 35 percent more likely to experience a breast cancer recurrence, compared with patients who did not drink alcohol, and a shocking 51 percent were more likely to die of the disease. Recurrence risk was highest among women who were postmenopausal, overweight, or obese. One biological explanation for this is that alcohol increases estrogen levels, as does obesity, and excess estrogen is associated with breast cancer.

  As for women who have not been diagnosed with breast cancer, research also suggests that in some women, as little as one drink per day can slightly raise the risk of invasive ductal carcinoma, a major form of breast cancer. Although it's impossible to know how alcohol will affect the risk of developing breast cancer in any individual woman, even a small increase in risk can make an impact.

- **Violent crime**: Heavy drinking increases a woman's risk of incurring a violent and sexual assault. If you pass out or black out, you are making yourself vulnerable to rape, STDs, unwanted pregnancies, and physical abuse. In 2002, a study in the *Journal of Studies on Alcohol* found that more than seventy thousand students between the ages of eighteen and twenty-four had been victims of alcohol-related sexual assault in the United States.

- **Liver disease**: Over the long term, women are more likely than men to develop alcoholic hepatitis (liver inflammation) and to die from cirrhosis of the liver. (See more on liver disease later in the chapter.)

- **Brain disease**: The brain, which contains a lot of water and needs a constant blood supply, is particularly vulnerable to the effects of alcohol. Most alcoholics have some loss of mental function, reduced brain size, and changes in the function of brain cells. Yet research suggests that women are more vulnerable than men to alcohol-induced brain damage. To a much lesser degree, beer, red wine, and vermouth can also trigger migraines, especially in women who are prone to these kinds of headaches.

- **Fetal alcohol syndrome (FAS) or fetal alcohol effects (FAE)**: If a woman drinks while pregnant, she risks giving birth to a child with developmental delays, organ dysfunction, facial abnormalities, epilepsy, poor motor skills, lack of concentration, and myriad behavioral problems, including hyperactivity, mental and social anxiety. It's estimated that each year in the United States, 1 in every 750 infants is born with a pattern of physical, developmental, and functional problems referred to as FAS, while another 40,000 are born with FAE. Children with FAE usually lack the distinctive FAS facial features and have normal IQs, so it is considered somewhat less serious than full-blown FAS.

  Although having a glass of wine while you're in the late stages of pregnancy probably won't harm your baby, even moderate alcohol intake, and especially periodic binge drinking, can seriously damage a developing nervous system, so the safest course is to abstain from drinking alcohol during your entire pregnancy.

- **Infertility**: Chronic heavy drinking can lead to menstrual problems that I will discuss more later on, as well as infertility and early menopause, according to a study on *Alcohol Research & Health* published in the NIAAA. Drinking during adolescence can also interfere with puberty, growth, and bone health.

- **Malnourishment**: It's not only drunkorexics who, if given the choice between a meal and a drink, will choose alcohol. The majority of female alcoholics are malnourished, as I was when I was drinking. Even though I had gained weight, when I checked into the treatment facility, doctors found that I was malnourished because eating had become secondary to my drinking.

In addition, the stomach lining can become irritated and burned by the abrasive chemicals in alcohol. Keep in mind that soldiers used alcohol to clean wounds when antiseptic wasn't available—imagine what it does to your stomach. Also, if you're throwing up, which alcoholics and certainly bulimics frequently do, the constant purging can destroy the enamel on your teeth, resulting in unsightly yellowing and tooth decay, the likes of which will cost thousands of dollars in dental work to repair if you haven't already spent all of your money on booze.

My Sister Died of Liver Disease at Fifty-Four, and the Doctors Said She Had the Body of a Ninety-Year-Old

Here is Anna's story of how alcohol robbed her sister of her youth and, ultimately, her life.

My sister died five years ago at age fifty-four of liver disease. She was the oldest of my four sisters, and she went from being the perfect child to the wild child. She started drinking in her teens, and I remember many family fights about her behavior. Not that my parents were teetotalers. The family rule was you never drank before 6 p.m. and you never drank during dinner, but between 6 and dinner you drank as fast and as hard as you could. Mind you, dinner for adults didn't start until 11:30 p.m. My family's cocktail of choice is vodka and 7-Up. And don't let anyone tell you that vodka has no odor—I could smell it coming out of my family's pores.

When Melinda went off to college, she joined a sorority and was able to drink unsupervised. She married another alcoholic after graduating, and they moved to Houston, where they had three children. Melinda tried to stop drinking a few times, but her husband wanted a drinking buddy. Her oldest daughter, Sally, would tell me how she'd come home from second grade to find her mother passed out on the bed.

Melinda's drinking was so bad that she kept getting fired from all her jobs, including as a Latin teacher in a private school, as a salesclerk, and another delivering pet supplies. Of course, if you asked her, it was always the employer's fault. The family moved to Chicago, where Melinda kept getting tickets for DUIs and finally flipped her MG convertible, and she was nearly killed.

That's when I got a call from my mother saying that I'd been elected to go to Chicago to put Melinda in a rehab. Her husband refused to do it, saying that she was fine, but the rest of us felt her car crash was a huge cry for help. I was living in New York and took a plane the next day to her house. I waited until the kids and the husband were gone before telling Melinda: "You have a drinking problem and you have got to go somewhere to get help. This can't go on." To my shock she said, "Okay."

We found a local hospital in Chicago where I dropped her off before returning home. We didn't tell anyone what we were doing. Not a note or a phone call—nothing. I don't know what her family must have thought happened. I was so focused on Melinda that I couldn't think of anything or anyone else. I realize now that I handled this terribly. I didn't know at the time, but in retrospect it was such a cavalier disregard for the children.

That rehab was supposed to last a month, but Melinda snuck out after ten days and went to a local bar. She was later found by Sally, unconscious and naked on her bed. The girl called me, asking what she should do, and I said, "Call 911." Melinda was kicked out of the program, of course, and went to another one, where she was once again told to leave. Melinda went in and out of rehabs for about a year until her insurance ran out.

My parents finally found a place in California that had a very high success rate. Again, it was a thirty-day program that had an additional sixty-day follow-up. This one seemed to work, and Melinda miraculously stayed sober for four years. During this period, I only saw her a few times because she stayed in California and never returned to her husband and children. Chicago was too much of a trigger for her. She was able to hold onto a receptionist job at a construction company while sober, but when we heard that she was fired, we knew that she had started drinking again.

It was New Year's Eve 2000 when she decided that she would have a sip of champagne to celebrate the new millennium. She was legally separated from her husband and was dating a guy who didn't know she was an alcoholic. They got engaged and moved to Arizona, where she started working as a hostess. Not surprisingly, she got fired from this job as well, although she denied that she was drinking again.

Things continued to spiral out of control, so Melinda called our parents and asked if she could come home and live with them. They agreed on the condition that she check herself into a nearby rehab, which she did. She walked out of rehab three days later and began verbally abusing my mother and father. My parents begged me to come over to help.

When I came, Melinda retreated into her room. We could hear her screaming incoherently there for hours. The only time she would come out would be to get a bottle of water from the freezer. We didn't understand where this crazy behavior was coming from because, as far as we knew, she had stopped drinking. I finally went into her room and saw this crazed look in her eyes.

What's going on with you?" I demanded, grabbing the water bottle from her hand. I took a sip and quickly spit it out because it was straight vodka. How stupid was I not to realize vodka doesn't freeze?

We got her into a rehab facility that day, which turned out to be her last. Within three months, she was in the hospital dying of liver disease. When I visited Melinda for the last time, the doctors were keeping her alive by pumping adrenaline into her heart, but she was already gone. We asked if we could donate anything to other sick patients, but the doctors said that not a single organ or part, including her skin and eyes, could be salvaged. Alcohol had given her the body of a ninety-year-old woman."

For some women, such as Melinda, the damage caused by drinking can eventually kill them. Others, such as Susan, whom you'll read about a little later, get to a point where they might want to end their lives. Susan narrowly escaped committing suicide, but her story embodies the hope that comes with recovery. Fortunately for her, facing the pain of her addiction head on prevented her from having a head-on collision and opened a door to the way out.

Liver Disease

Many alcoholics suffer from alcohol-induced liver disease. If you are one of them, know that there are treatment options available, according to Memorial Sloane Kettering in New York, depending on how extensive the damage and your general health. Please consult a doctor immediately should symptoms occur, such as a yellowish pigmentation of the skin and in the whites of your eyes. Following are a few scenarios that may occur if you have been diagnosed with liver disease:

- A tumor is found in one area and can be removed.
- A tumor is found in one area but cannot be totally removed safely.
- The cancer has spread throughout the liver and/or to other parts of the body.
- The cancer has reoccurred in the liver or in another part of the body after initial treatment.
- There is extensive liver cirrhosis or liver failure that prevents surgical treatment of the tumor.

Depending on the stage of the disease and other factors, such as the extent of cirrhosis and liver failure, your treatment team will determine the most appropriate therapy, which may include surgery, minimally invasive therapies, chemotherapy and/or biological therapy, and radiation therapy.

Physical Assault

Many women get raped or are physically assaulted while drunk, which may result in a desire to medicate the emotional pain from the trauma with alcohol. It is sad that the answer to a short-term solution so often becomes a long-term problem, but the pain and shame that women feel afterward can add fuel to the fire of their addiction.

I Didn't Think It Could Ever Happen to Me

Maggie, a thirty-three-year-old doctoral student living in Dallas, Texas, tells how her drinking led to the worst thing that could ever happen to her: rape.

I come from a solidly middle-class, close-knit family of Southern Baptists who went to church on Sunday. I had a happy childhood, and I had always excelled at school and sports. I began to experiment with alcohol when I was about thirteen after my parents had gotten a divorce.

When I was in high school, I went to a party with some older kids and drank too much trashcan punch, which is Hawaiian Punch mixed with liquor. I grew up in a dry county, but you could get liquor from local bootleggers who sold to minors. I got gang-raped at the party by some guys who followed me into the bathroom. The only one who I knew was a guy who found me in the bathroom afterward. He picked me up and carried me out of the party and took me home.

I didn't tell anyone what happened to me. The guys who raped me were seniors who went to my high school, so I had to pass them in the halls. I just went into survival mode. My memory of that night was a bit foggy because of the alcohol and the trauma. I remember going home and going straight to bed. The next morning my mother said, "You were drunk last night."

"Yes, I was," I admitted, adding nothing more.

"Don't let it happen again," she warned. And with that, we just went on with our lives. She had no idea, of course, that I had been sexually assaulted. Now this event could have gone two ways for me. I could have told myself, "Bad things happen when you drink," or do what I did, which was use the shame of what happened as a reason to drink more. There was too much pain to handle in my life, from the rape to my parents' divorce to the general angst I felt as a teenager.

And so I began to drink heavily and more frequently. My friends were all drinking, too, at the time, but my drinking was getting out of hand, to the point where some of my friends went to my mom to tell her that they were concerned about me. My mother thought I was drinking because of the divorce. So she got me into counseling. I was fifteen. I didn't like the counselor, who was an authoritative man with a Christian perspective that didn't resonate with me at the time. He was domineering, and I had some anger issues with males. We just didn't bond, and he told my mother not to bother bringing me back.

When I was a junior in high school, I decided to stop drinking. I got involved with church and tried to do what I thought was the right thing. I started preparing for college and writing applications. I was in the 90th percentile and got into every college I applied to, so I managed to keep my grades up, despite what was going on. I always did well in school, which prompted me to continue drinking. I never drank and drove, and I didn't get in trouble with the law or have some of the negative consequences that my peers experienced. My mother knew I was still drinking, but I convinced her that I was only doing what all the other kids were doing.

Things starting getting bad again during my senior year of high school. I drank every weekend and sometimes on week nights. I started to drop out of things. I quit the golf team and choir, both of which were important to me. I stopped participating in other sports as well. I started getting into harder drugs, like cocaine. I needed something that would give me the level of intoxication I wanted. I was also still trying to repress what had happened to me. Sometimes I would drink until I blacked out and started crying and telling people about the rape. I never remembered doing this, and telling my peers didn't help because they didn't know what to do with this information.

After graduating in the top five of my class, I got an honors scholarship to Tulane in New Orleans. I had a lot of hopes and dreams for my future. I hoped that I could start fresh at college, and I vowed not to drink or do drugs. I had to uphold a certain GPA if I was to keep my scholarship. I managed to keep it together for the first year, but I began to get into trouble again with my drinking. I got alcohol poisoning at one of the fraternity parties. I told the school nurses that someone put something in my drink, but I got written up for alcohol poisoning. I was asked to speak to the head resident. I apologized, but I still never told anyone about what happened, except when I was in a blackout stupor.

Because I was using alcohol as my primary coping tool, I started having some negative consequences. My drinking and drugs affected my relationships with my roommate and with men. I didn't date a lot, and I'm still not in a relationship. I went on a bender and tore up our dorm room and yelled and screamed. My roommate finally said, "I can't take it anymore. I tried to be nice and understanding, but you have to leave." I got written up again and moved to another room.

There are a lot of people who drink and get happy. I wasn't that kind of drunk. I would fight with people or end up raging, sobbing, and sorrowful. I used the drugs to prevent these emotions from coming on when I drank.

I was now in trouble with the university, and I was referred to the drug and alcohol counseling program. Again, it didn't really help. The counselor there suggested I go to an outpatient treatment or twelve-step program, neither of which I did. They threatened to kick me out of school, but I didn't believe them. A lot of my friends whom I partied with began flunking out. One day their parents would come pick them up, and they'd be gone. When I think about my friends at Tulane, only three graduated out of ten. But I kept plugging on until I couldn't maintain the GPA I needed to keep my scholarship and had to leave.

I didn't want to move back with my mom, so I got an apartment in another town and continued to drink and smoke pot. I decided to take out some student loans and return to college with a renewed sense of commitment to cut down on my drinking and drugs. I resolved only to drink on the weekends, but my weekends would begin on Thursday afternoon and continue to Sunday night. I'd be so tired on Monday that I couldn't go to class until Tuesday and Wednesday, after which it was Thursday, and my weekend would start all over again.

I started writing hot checks and getting my electricity turned off when I couldn't pay the bills, disengaging from my family, and getting into fights with people. All this made me want to drink more, and I essentially became a master chemist with my body. I was up to over half of a bottle of scotch a day and using coke to keep me from passing out. At the time, I weighed around 110 pounds.

I started taking antianxiety pills so I wouldn't have to drink as much. I got the shakes, sometimes in the middle of night. I thought I was simply dehydrated. On my twenty-first birthday, there was a big tropical storm headed for New Orleans, and they evacuated the city. I went to stay at a friend's mother's house. Typically, I got drunk, took some pills, and did cocaine. I lost it and collapsed into a sobbing mess, confessing everything to my friend's mother. It was the first time I had told an adult what had happened in high school. The next day, she sat down with me and said, "Do you have recollection of last night?" I didn't, but I said I was sorry if I did anything horrible.

She said, "I'm not going to say anything about this again, but I care about you, and you really need to get some help."

The next day my mother called and accused me of stealing her medication during my visit. Ironically, it wasn't me because they were drugs I didn't do, but I couldn't convince her. It turned out one of her friends was addicted to prescription drugs and had been coming into her house and raiding her medicine cabinet. When she got caught, she went into treatment. I thought if it worked for her, maybe I'd give it a try. She got clean.

But I still wasn't ready. In 1998, I ended up blacking out at the New Orleans airport. Apparently, I had stumbled up to a flight attendant and said I didn't know where I was supposed to go. She strapped me into the seat where the flight attendants usually sit and I passed out. After we landed, they called my sister, who drove me to my mother's house. When I woke up, I was a sobbing mess. I apologized, but this time I said, "I have a plan." I drove over to my mother's friend's house and asked her about her treatment. She was really supportive but gave me only until Saturday night to make a decision. I was too sick, she said, to go on much longer.

I checked myself into a rehab facility, but not before going to one more party, where I ended up getting into a fight with a friend, hitting her, and driving her car out into the middle of the field and throwing away her car keys. When she called me the next day to ask for her keys, I didn't remember a thing. I knew that if I went back to school after this, I would never make it out alive.

I sat down with my mom and said, "I have a drug and alcohol problem, and I need to get help." I told her about the sexual assault. She said, "Okay, I don't have the money to help you, but your grandfather does. You are going to have to tell him the truth. And this is going to be your last chance to go to a good facility."

It took eight days before I could be released in the general population. I had the sweats, the shakes, and high blood pressure. The entire treatment took forty-five days, but it worked, and I've been sober twelve years. I never went back to Tulane, but I'm finishing my doctorate in human development at a local university.

To girls who have been assaulted, I say, tell someone who can help you. And it doesn't matter how drunk or high you were, it is never your fault. Don't blame yourself, like I did. There are people out there who can help—no one should suffer in silence.

Even if you don't have cuts, scrapes, or bruises, rape is an extremely serious psychological trauma. No one should go through the horror of rape alone. You're probably going to need professional counseling, as well as the support of your friends and family. Even if you blacked out, do not blame yourself for the assault.

Like Maggie, many rape victims find it difficult to ask for help because the rape has made them feel ashamed, weak, and wounded. If it's hard for you to ask for help, here's what to do. Pick a special friend and ask that friend to help you find more help. Ask that special friend to help you think of other people who would be good for different kinds of help. Ask your friend to make the phone calls for you.

You don't have to tell your support people every detail. The people you ask for help don't have to be experts on rape, but they should be people you trust. Have a support person accompany you to appointments, meetings, and discussions pertaining to the rape. Never go alone, whether it's to a doctor's appointment or to the police station. In fact, it's a good idea to have someone by your side even when you're making phone calls about what happened to you. Having someone accompany you will help you remember information, and he or she can remind you about which questions you wanted to ask. It's also a good idea to ask the person who's with you to take notes because you will probably be highly emotional when recounting the events and are likely to forget details or important information.

Made a Plan to Get Really Drunk and Drive into a Concrete Wall

Twenty-eight-year-old Susan talks about how drinking nearly ruined her life.

I grew up in St. Louis with parents who did everything possible to give my brother and me a good childhood. My dad was a steelworker who traveled a lot for work. We lived in an upper-middle-class town, but we were a working-class family.

I had always romanticized alcohol as something people drank at parties to have fun. I never saw negative consequences from people drinking. I remember saying to myself that I couldn't wait until I was old enough to start drinking. The first time I drank, I was in the sixth grade on the playground blacktop of my middle school. A friend had a bottle of Wild Turkey that she stole from her parents, and we both took some swigs from it. It was disgusting, but I wanted to get that good feeling. I also used to steal those little airplane bottles of liquor that my father would bring home.

When I was in high school, my drinking progressed because I had greater access to liquor. I would drink anything I could get my hands on, mostly after school. Amazingly, I was still able to keep up my grades. I was involved in drama club, too, so I was always able to put on a good front—until I turned fifteen. That's when I got pregnant.

Having to tell my parents and seeing the disappointment on their faces was devastating. It was the first time I felt the consequences of my drinking and realized what a failure I was. It kills me to this day, and I've blocked out a lot of what happened. I remember my mother saying that I would have to stop smoking, but when she saw me smoking out on the porch, she said, "Well, I guess you made your decision." I ended up having an abortion.

I drank so much after that because I couldn't handle the pain and remorse. When we went to the clinic, I sneaked a peak at the ultrasound in my file, which made it even harder. As I got older, I kept thinking about how old the baby would be. I was in an abusive relationship with the baby's father. He kept me isolated and wouldn't allow me to have friends. He went with me to the abortion clinic, but he got high as soon as we got home. Once while I was still living with him, I had to go to the hospital because I kept throwing up for three days, and I got severely dehydrated. I don't remember much about this time, but my body was shutting down.

We stayed together for a year after that, mostly because of the drugs and alcohol, but I left him after he started cheating on me. I was using heavy drugs when we were together but stopped after we broke up. I went to five high schools during this period. I thought if I changed schools, I would stop drinking, but I'd just find a new group of friends who liked to drink, and it would start all over again. I wanted so badly to fit in. I wanted to feel pretty, and I just couldn't handle all those things that teenagers go through. I didn't drink because I wanted to be cool, but because I wanted to be happy, and I thought alcohol could make that happen.

After I broke up with my boyfriend, I moved back with my parents and quit drinking cold turkey. I detoxed on my own for about a month. I wanted so badly to be that good girl again. I was diagnosed with ADHD, and the doctors put me on Adderall. I stopped eating and got really thin from the medication. I was so good at hiding what was going on that no one really knew how bad it was. It became my new drug, and I drank on top of it. I drank mostly on the weekends at this point because I didn't want to cause my parents any more shame and pain.

I finally graduated high school with really good grades and wanted to go into architecture. I decided to go to a community college and transfer later to a four-year school. That summer I thought that I was sober for good. My one childhood friend, who had always stuck by me, was going to another university, and she took me to a fraternity party. I liked the kids there and started drinking again every weekend at these parties.

That's when the negative consequences returned. I was driving drunk, and I started running into curbs and blowing out tires. I wasn't afraid of having an accident but about using my money to fix my car that I would rather spend on alcohol. It was a vicious cycle of driving drunk, blowing out tires, fixing the car, and trying to scrounge up money for more alcohol. I did get pulled over once when I was insanely drunk, and there were even open containers of liquor in my car. The cop asked me where I was going, but he looked at my address on my license and said, "Okay, please get home safe. You're a good girl from a good area." So he let me go. I was eighteen and underage. I should have gone to jail that night. Somehow I always managed to skirt the line and get away with things.

During this time, I was working my way through school and still managing to get good grades. I looked great on paper, but I was a mess. I started drinking vodka every night. The reason I switched to vodka was because it took so much beer for me to get drunk that my body couldn't handle it—I'd just start throwing up. Years later I lost the enamel on my teeth and had to have nine root canals and $15,000 of dental work, which I paid for with the money I earned working at a UPS store. The dentists thought I was bulimic.

I continued to spiral down, coming home drunk and throwing up. My mom went through hell whenever I'd disappear for days. She finally said I couldn't come home if I was drunk. I ended up sleeping in my car. Everyone in the neighborhood would pass me in the morning, which caused my parents even more embarrassment.

I kept drinking and hooking up with guys until I turned twenty-one. I used protection because I was afraid of getting pregnant again. A girl I worked with who was in AA kept trying to get me to go to meetings with her. I finally gave in just to shut her up. I related to the people there but decided I wouldn't get sober before my twenty-first birthday. I wanted to party my heart out because I would finally be legal and not have to use the fake IDs. When my birthday came, I drank and drank and drank but couldn't get drunk. All my friends left because they were sick of dealing with me. I went with a guy to his car and blacked out. Luckily, nothing happened. All I could remember was the smell of his leather seats.

I had never blacked out before, and it terrified me. I was fortunate that this guy didn't take advantage of me. I decided the next day that I would only drink at home. I bought bottles of vodka daily, which would last me two days. That's all I did the summer I turned twenty-one. In August, I had a moment of clarity.

I couldn't remember the last time I had been sober. Everything was still okay on the outside, but I was falling apart on the inside. I couldn't take it anymore. I made a plan to get really drunk and drive into a concrete wall, so it wouldn't look like a suicide.

One night I got drunk enough, but instead of getting into a car I called the girl who took me to the AA meeting. That was 2003, and I stopped drinking the next day for good. We poured all the alcohol I had in my house down the drain together. I know that had I not made that call, I would have been dead within a year.

I'm now happily married and seven years sober. I transferred to the University of Washington in St. Louis, where I got a degree in architecture. I never thought I would be able to love myself, no less find someone who would love me.

HOW TO TALK TO AN ALCOHOLIC

In my years as a counselor, I have worked with hundreds of alcoholic women in crisis. Many of them were looking for someone who would talk them off the ledge or off the sauce. If you don't have someone like this in your life, seek professional help. In the meantime, here are some tips for what you should and shouldn't do:

- Stay calm, talk slowly, and use reassuring tones.
- Ask simple questions, such as, "What's going on with you right now?" Repeat them if necessary, using the same words each time.
- Don't take your loved one's actions or hurtful words personally.
- Say, "I'm here. I care. I want to help. How can I help you?"
- Resist the urge to be glib by saying things such as, "It's your own fault," "Get over it," or "Stop acting crazy."
- Don't handle the crisis alone. Call family, friends, neighbors, people from your place of worship, or people from a local support group to help you.
- Don't threaten to call 911 unless you mean it. When you call 911, police and/or an ambulance are likely to come to your house. This may make your loved ones more upset,

so use 911 only when you or someone else is in immediate danger.

Relational Consequences

"One reason I don't drink is that I want to know when I am having a good time."
—*Lady Astor*

Although your health takes a huge hit when you hit the bottle, another enormous consequence of drinking is the toll it takes on your relationships and family. The problem occurs because you are no longer present, and alcohol becomes your first and foremost love interest. It becomes your primary focus, your friend, your confidant, and what gets you through the day. It is the central organizing factor of your life.

You might start to cancel your lunch dates with friends or make sure you go somewhere that serves drinks. Perhaps you yell, curse out, or even fight with your partner, friends, or anyone within spitting distance. Mothers can neglect their children, forget to pick them up at school, or be unable to cook them proper meals. Some become verbally and physically abusive. There's a real sense of disconnect. When you miss your child's school play or show up drunk and embarrass your kids in front of their friends, it is a hurt that can cut even deeper than physical mistreatment. It's also a memory that they (and you) will never forget.

I Never Thought I Would Lose Control Over My Life the Way I Did

Fortunately, as sixty-year-old Cheryl's story reveals, there is always hope for those who choose to recover.

I was in the holding cell and called my brother to bail me out. . . . My car wasn't the only thing that was a total wreck.

I grew up in rural Texas in a religious family where drinking was taboo. My mother was an extremely domineering woman who liked to control my life. In high school I was a cheerleader voted most popular, most beautiful, most musical, most everything, but I felt like a fake. She wanted me to marry my high school boyfriend, who I wasn't in love with. I stayed with him only to please my mother.

Inside, I was miserable, but no one knew. I was a good girl who never drank or had sex or did anything bad. The first time I drank was on my senior trip to Acapulco, where I tried a tequila drink. I didn't get drunk, but I liked the way it made me feel. I went to college, where I got an education degree, as my parents insisted, even though I wanted to major in piano performance.

Here I was, the most sheltered girl on the planet exposed to a whole new world! A bunch of us in the dorm went to a drive-in movie and drank a bottle of Ripple. I had a blast! When I told my parents I was breaking up with my high school boyfriend, they threatened to take me out of school. I remember falling on the bed, weeping in distress, but, thankfully, they let me stay.

My freshman year in college I met a football player who asked me on a date. It was my nineteenth birthday, and we out and drank rum and coke. This time I got wasted. I went back to my room and threw up in a wastebasket. My mother decided I should move into an apartment off campus with another girl. The day I moved, I met and started dating a guy who I fell head over heels in love with. He was one of five brothers, and his mother was a recovering alcoholic. We got married when I was a sophomore. My grades went to hell in a handbasket, but I managed to stay in school. My husband and I stayed together for about a year before getting divorced. I got my grades back up, but I was dating and drinking a lot. At this point, whenever I drank, I'd get wasted.

That year I went to a geology lab in college, where I fell in love with a dashing teaching assistant. He got his Ph.D. and moved to New Orleans, where he was from, to work for an oil company. He got drunk one night and asked me to marry him. Now, I'm twenty-two and in my second marriage. We went out to a restaurant one night, and I got drunk and fell down a flight of stairs.

He introduced me to his parents, who were also alcoholics. I remember his mother telling me that I should switch to vodka so "no one could smell it." She was my alcoholic mentor. Whenever we got together with his family, we would start with Champagne, move on to Bloody Marys, beer, and then vodka. We'd all be under the table by the evening. I lived in New Orleans for eight years, drinking vodka martinis at night while my husband drank Scotch. I'd have about two to three a night, but I wasn't even getting high.

This marriage was bad from the start. My husband wanted a buddy more than a wife. I see now that he was probably gay. He wasn't really interested in sex—at least, with me. There was no happiness in my life, and vodka was my only friend. Thank goodness, he didn't want kids, because I couldn't imagine going nine months without vodka. When I went with him on business trips to South America, I'd sit there at the bar by myself, using the only Spanish I know, which was, "Do you have any ice?"

I decided to take a course at Tulane. I would carry a little bottle of vodka with me to school and sneak a drink in the library stacks. I was so terribly unhappy, and I was hiding my liquor because my husband didn't want me drinking. I'd hide it in my vacuum cleaner, under the mattress, and in a Scope mouthwash bottle, where I'd disguise it with green food coloring.

I started getting into car accidents. My husband finally put me into a treatment center in New Orleans, but I still refused to believe that I was an alcoholic. I was convinced that I could control my drinking. I played the game and pretended, but I had no intention of going through life without vodka. Of course, this made me feel even worse about myself. As soon as I got out of rehab, I bought a bottle of vodka.

I didn't realize I had a drinking problem until I was supposed to go to a piano recital for one of my students and I was too drunk to show up. My husband said he couldn't take it anymore and kicked me out of the house. I moved to west Texas, where I got a job as an elementary school teacher—still drinking, of course, but not during school. I remember one day I was carpooling with another teacher who had to pull over so I could throw up.

There's no word to describe the humiliation and the hatred that I felt for myself. My mother suggested I speak to my minister, Ted, about my depression. I agreed, but as I walked out the door she said, "Don't tell him how much you drink."

She thought I was depressed about my failed marriages, but I was simply drinking because I hated myself and my life, although I felt like a failure. I walked into Ted's office and immediately started wailing and telling him about how much I drink. He listened calmly and then said, "Let's talk about treatment." He recommended Dr. Tom, a former priest in recovery. I credit Dr. Tom and Ted with saving my life.

This was my second time in rehab. I knew I was an alcoholic, but I thought I could stop if I wanted to. My mother had controlled everything in my life, and alcohol was a friend that I refused to give up. I couldn't fathom life without vodka. I would go to AA meetings and sit in the corner, drunk. I would black out for hours at a time—all the time.

One day I was drinking vodka and got into a car wreck. It wasn't serious, and I managed to flirt my way out of a ticket because I don't look like what some might think is a typical alcoholic. But before too long, I got into another car accident. I wasn't so lucky this time, and I was taken down to the station. I was in the holding cell and called my brother to come bail me out. His friend, who I was dating, came too, and I apologized to both of them and swore I would never do this again. I was twenty-nine years old, and the car wasn't the only thing that was a total wreck.

Not long after that accident, I bought a bottle of vodka and chugged the whole thing. I remember waking up in the emergency room, trying to pull out my catheters. Dr. Tom, the former priest, said that I had broken a record for having the highest level of alcohol of anyone ever admitted to that hospital who survived. My aunt came to visit me, and I sobbed, "What's wrong with me?"

She said, "Honey, your mother never wanted us to tell you this, but there are a lot of alcoholics in your family." She started rattling off names of family members who had drinking problems.

I went into treatment at the hospital after that. Ted came to see me every day. He would hug me and say, "You can do it." I wanted to do it, but I still didn't know how I could live without drinking. While I was in treatment, I worked through a lot of my issues with my mother. I went to after-care and kept seeing Dr. Tom, but still I kept drinking. I just couldn't stop.

My boyfriend finally said, "I love you, but I've got to get away from this. You are killing yourself, and I don't know how to stop you." I felt even more remorse and self-hatred for having failed once again with a relationship. I was still going to AA, and Dr. Tom would sit with me and smile and say, "Don't worry, you will get it." I continued to drink until one night I went out to a bar near my apartment. I have no memory of how I got home, but when I came to, I was covered in vomit. I knew that people can choke on their own vomit and thought, "Is this how I'm going to die?" That was the day, thirty years ago, that I stopped drinking.

I started going to AA meetings three or four times a day. I got a job working for a beer company. Odd choice for an alcoholic, I know, but it was God's way of testing me. No one I worked with knew that I had a drinking problem. Every day beer was right there in front of me, but I never touched a drop. I drank soda and kept my AA book in my purse.

After two years of sobriety, my boyfriend saw that I was serious about not drinking, and he asked me to marry him. I now have two children, who know all about my history. Drinking was a way for me to cover my pain and to relieve my depression and self-hatred. To other women who might be wondering whether they have the strength to stop, I say what Dr. Tom said to me: "You will get it. Never give up. If I can sober up, anyone can!"

The pain many women experience while drinking can wreak havoc on their families, causing the drinkers to either leave or be kicked out of their homes. When this happens, the painful feelings of alienation and detachment from friends and loved ones will inevitably drive women deeper into alcoholism.

The Turning Point for Me Was When My Best Friend Didn't Invite Me to Her Birthday Party

Drinking nearly destroyed thirty-three-year-old Grace's life as she tells it here.

I first started sipping my mom's Budweiser when I was nine. By the time I was ten, I was drinking Scotch before mellowing out to watch cartoons. I come from a fairly affluent family—my father is a lawyer, and my mother is a business manager. I always looked up to my mom and sisters, who were happy drinkers without alcohol problems. I started because I was curious about what it would be like to drink, and there was also an element of doing something that was forbidden. Unlike my mother, my dad was a miserable alcoholic, who was an angry drunk. I equated alcoholism with my dad and successful drinking with my mom. I wanted to be like my mom but ended up being exactly like my dad.

In addition to sneaking Dewars from my parents' liquor cabinet, I would drink cough medicine. Even though I started drinking when I was still a kid, I didn't get drunk until I was fourteen, when I had older friends and more access to alcohol. When I was fifteen, my parents sent me to psychologists to figure out what was wrong with me. They had no idea that I was drinking and bingeing. I was diagnosed with attention deficit hyperactivity disorder (ADHD), and that's when the Ritalin, Adderall, and dexedrine starting coming. I would abuse the pills if I couldn't get my hands on alcohol. I loved the pills because I could take them while I was drinking, which would help me function in high school. The combination of depressants and stimulants would even me out.

I was super depressed in high school. I had really bad acne, lied, stole, and made terrible decisions with boys. I had one serious boyfriend, but I could never remain faithful when I was drinking. But I never got into trouble because I was best friends with the principal's daughter.

I started having blackouts when I was a freshman at college in South Carolina. I was really depressed in college, so I was put on antidepressants. Every time I took them with alcohol, I would have blackouts, where I'd wake up not knowing where I was, where my car was, and why people were mad at me. My first semester, when I was eighteen, I tried to quit for one day so I could study for a test. I remember looking down at my textbook, shaking and breaking out into cold sweats. I couldn't function, and I crawled into the bathroom and started dry heaving. I told my roommate that I thought I needed a beer. She gave me one, and I was fine. That's how bad my physical addiction was.

I managed to stay out of trouble because my father was an attorney, and whenever I was stopped by police for speeding I never got charged for anything, and there were pills, cocaine, and medication in the car. I had an accident, and the cops did an alcohol breath test, but when my dad showed up, I didn't get arrested.

I eventually dropped out of college my second semester sophomore year and moved back in with my parents. One night I came home drunk at 2 a.m., and I got into a fight with my mom about my drinking and started choking her. Like my father, I had a horrible temper when drunk. I would pick fights with women at bars, punch windows and walls with my fists. My dad and brother came home and pulled me off. They kicked me out of the house, and I took all the money out of my bank account, which came to about $500, and was homeless for a while, living on friends' couches. I was nineteen.

I got a job at a fast-food place and continued drinking, mostly whiskey and tequila, but pretty much anything I could get my hands on. Somehow I was promoted to manager, but I would drink with my fellow employees. I would hide a pint of vodka in my car for on the way to school. All my friends were into drinking and drugs, too. All my "good" friends had long left me by then.

When I was twenty, I met a guy and moved in with him. We followed a band for a while, living like hippies. My apartment was a mess, and I was miserable. I had no idea what being happy meant. I felt spiritually empty. A void. I remember trying to talk to God and being with nature and animals. I was brought up Catholic and had always longed to be closer to God, but I was so full of shame and guilt for the way I was that I felt hopeless.

The turning point for me was when my best friend since I was five didn't invite me to her birthday party. I was really upset and felt more alone that night than ever before. I went to a bar and got into another fight, so they kicked me out, and I went home and my boyfriend also kicked me out. I tried breaking into his house, and I kept falling down and screaming until someone called the police.

My brother came to bring me home, and I remember wanting to kill myself. My mother said I called and asked for help. She came over with my brother, father, and some friends she met at Al-Anon and AA. My father had been sober for a few years. They all kind of ambushed me. They asked me if I was ready to quit drinking. I said yes, and it was like a huge weight was lifted. They said, "Are you ready to go to treatment?" and I said, "Absolutely not."

I was dry for two years after that by going to AA meetings. I celebrated my twenty-first birthday sober. I fell in love with the program but didn't really take it that seriously. I thought all I needed to do was to get the alcohol out of my body, but I never replaced it with anything. I still went to bars to play pool with friends, but I didn't drink. I was young, and I still wanted to have fun.

I started having anxiety attacks again, and my obsession to drink was returning. I went for three months feeling suicidal, until I checked myself into a hospital. I was in the rehab for five weeks, where I learned about the disease of alcohol, which set me free. The major breakthrough I had there was that there was a higher power, which brought me to my knees. I remembered how angry my father was when he was drunk and realized I was exactly like him. My father found a replacement for alcohol and is now happy—I needed one, too.

I got involved with the twelve-step program, which I resisted at first, and now I practice my own personal spirituality that doesn't involve going to church but is a combination of different philosophies that make sense to me. I said, "Okay, God, if you're out there, help me!" I don't know what God is, but to me it's unconditional love. Since then, I went back to college and got a master's degree. I'm now married, with a stepson, and I'm helping other people in recovery.

WHAT IS ADHD?

Attention deficit hyperactivity disorder (ADHD) affects about 3 to 5 percent of school-age children. ADHD may run in families, but it is not clear exactly what causes it. Whatever the cause may be, imaging studies suggest that the brains of children with ADHD are different from those of other children. Depression, lack of sleep, learning disabilities, tic disorders, and behavior problems may be confused with, or appear with, ADHD. Anyone suspected of having ADHD should be examined by a doctor to rule out other physical or psychological problems. Most children with ADHD also have at least one other developmental or behavioral problem.

What Are the Symptoms of ADHD?

The symptoms of ADHD fall into three groups:

1. Lack of attention (inattentiveness)
2. Hyperactivity
3. Impulsive behavior (impulsivity)

Some children with ADHD primarily have the inattentive type; others may have a combination of types. Those with the inattentive type are less disruptive and are more likely not to be diagnosed with ADHD.

Inattentive Symptoms

- Fails to give close attention to details or makes careless mistakes in schoolwork

- Has difficulty keeping attention during tasks or play
- Does not seem to listen when spoken to directly
- Does not follow through on instructions and fails to finish schoolwork, chores, or duties in the workplace
- Has difficulty organizing tasks and activities
- Avoids or dislikes tasks that require sustained mental effort (such as schoolwork)
- Often loses toys, assignments, pencils, books, or tools needed for tasks or activities
- Is easily distracted
- Is often forgetful in daily activities

Hyperactivity Symptoms

- Fidgets with hands or feet or squirms in seat
- Leaves seat when remaining seated is expected
- Runs about or climbs in inappropriate situations
- Has difficulty playing quietly
- Is often "on the go," acts as if "driven by a motor," talks excessively

Impulsivity Symptoms

- Blurts out answers before questions have been completed
- Has difficulty awaiting his or her turn
- Interrupts or intrudes on others (butts into conversations or games)

Legal Consequences

The legal consequences of drinking can happen to any alcoholic, but they occur most often to those who drink in public, as opposed to the closet drinker, who is more likely to drink at home. Age and maturity also help women make better decisions, such as not driving while intoxicated, although those deep in the throes of alcoholism will ignore their better judgment.

In addition to drunk driving, which can end tragically, one of the worst things that can happen to a woman is to have her children taken away. Being an "unfit mother" means that you have relinquished your most cherished duty in life, which is caring for and protecting your children. The guilt and shame that come with giving up your children is so great that for recovery specialists such as me, it is more difficult to help these women to get and to stay sober. That said, having children makes it even more important that you do so.

I Lost the Custody of My Children to My Ex-Boyfriend

Dee tells the horrible story of how her alcoholism caused her to lose her children.

I was absolutely despondent after having tossed out eight months of sobriety for one afternoon of drinking with friends. There was a lot at stake at that time, and it resulted in my losing my two youngest children to my estranged ex-boyfriend in an emergency custody hearing and then some time later losing custody entirely!

We had been in the midst of a custody battle, and I was desperate to find some help. I just couldn't face the idea of going back to AA, although AA had been kind to me before. I drank for nearly thirty years, with many long stretches of sobriety, mostly on my own, a couple of times with AA/NA, for each of my pregnancies and when the babies were infants and a few other approximately year-long stretches. Oh, I also did lots of drugs from a very early age, most notably and damaging, crack, but that was something I was able to give up many years ago. Alcohol became my fixture and the thing I went back to over and over.

I was terrified of the time commitment of AA and that it would take away the little visiting time I had with my children. I felt like there had to be a better way, so I Googled and found SMART Recovery. The boards utterly fascinated me, and after some time, I worked up my courage to both post and try out an online meeting.

I was so scared! I had never been in a chat room or posted anywhere publicly. I was hugely drawn to the genuine warmth, kindness, and compassion I found there. I'm not very good at asking for help. I wanted what I saw others giving and getting, particularly on the message boards, and so I found some courage and started posting every day on one of the check-in threads. I started attending all the meetings. I ultimately became involved in volunteering.

I went through some difficult things with that custody battle and also lost my regular job (not related to drinking), but I found a huge amount of support here throughout. I got pretty good at facilitating (totally surprising to me). I gradually learned how to find comfort in being me. I made very good progress for about eighteen months and then started to have some difficulties after I lost my custody battle. I felt strong in not drinking but lonely.

I had a brief lapse shortly after that and have had approximately six-month stretches of sobriety since. I feel comfortable with the sober part. What I was not so comfortable with were my relationships, the need for approval, fear, and anger. When things were going smoothly and I had a lot going on in my life, I was okay. When things got tough emotionally, I still didn't really know how to cope. I continue to struggle with these things, but I feel like I've had many breakthroughs.

During my last major lapse, I even started smoking crack again for a few weeks, off and on—something I hadn't done in over thirteen years! Now that was a shocker! Depression has been a factor for me, as well as feeling overwhelmed by loss. I continue to find new things and new ways to look at my world and new healthier ways to cope with my life. I am learning to care for myself. I am learning to give of myself without expectations in return. I am learning to forgive and accept others, including myself. I am learning to enjoy my life as a whole, as well as the little moments.

If you have lost your children due to alcoholism but have since recovered and have been deemed medically and mentally capable of regaining custody of your kids, you must find good legal counsel. Take extra time to do the research so that you get the best lawyer for your individual situation, and make sure to get references.

A good lawyer will be more than happy to share references with you, but don't call only the people whom he or she provides. Find other clients who have used the attorney's services. Call at least three of them, and compare your case with theirs. Obviously, you need someone who specializes in child custody cases, so make sure your attorney is a certified family law specialist. This ensures that he or she has had the training and experience that you need.

Work Consequences

"If drinking is interfering with your work, you're probably a heavy drinker. If work is interfering with your drinking, you're probably an alcoholic."
—Unknown

Approximately 77 percent of all drug and alcohol abusers are employed. Not only does substance abuse pose a danger to you, especially if you operate machinery or vehicles, it presents a risk to fellow employees, customers, and innocent bystanders. According to the National Association of Treatment Providers, alcohol use alone accounts for an 86 percent loss in business profits, as well as an astounding five hundred million missed workdays each year.

Although this is probably the least painful consequence for women, who do not define themselves as much as men do by their careers, losing a job due to alcoholism can cause your life to collapse like a house of cards. Women, especially those who are single wage earners, depend on their jobs to care for themselves and their families or to pay their rent or mortgages. If you can't sober up and find another job, you are only a few bounced checks away from being homeless and destitute. Ask any woman what her worst fear is, aside from the loss of her children, and she will probably say becoming a bag lady.

For those who have invested years and tens of thousands of dollars on a college education, you are giving up on a dream. I nearly threw away my hope of getting a doctorate because of my drinking, but recovery allowed me to eventually fulfill that dream. For professional women, their identities, as well as their ability to support themselves, are strongly tied up in their jobs. The following women's stories show how alcohol can send you into a further spiral if you risk losing your source of income and can no longer support yourself or, if you have one, your family.

Lost Business

I had a small cleaning business for a couple of years. Then I started to drink too much, too early, and canceled too many jobs due to being too drunk to drive there or clean once I got there. The cleaning businesses gradually died. I know I'd worked drunk a lot of times. I wonder what they thought of me. I know what I thought of myself.

—Anonymous

When you get up each morning to go to work, ask whatever higher power you believe in to help you have another sober day. When you go to bed each night, thank that same power for another sober day.

Absent from Work

I had vowed for years that if I get fired over my drinking, I'll quit drinking. I missed work on Friday—too drunk to be awakened by my alarm clock. That was a first for me.

I drank all weekend, got fired on Monday morning, went to an AA meeting at noon, though I didn't stop drinking then.

I got rehired on Wednesday with evening hours. This sort of thing happens when you work in the hospitality industry. A few months later, to protect my fragile sobriety, I switched to an office job. Less money, less stress, zero tolerance for drinkers.

—Carol

Sometimes stressful jobs will add to your desire to drink. Mine certainly did! When this is the case, it is a better to take a lower-paying or lower-status position, as Carol did, if it means getting off the hamster wheel of anxiety and stops you from drinking to cope with your pain.

Coming to Work Drunk

Lost a great job. Missed too much time. Showed up either still drunk or smelling like booze.

—Gemmie

If you go to work smelling of booze, it's only a matter of time before you get canned. Taking too many sick days is also a red flag that alcohol is more important to you than your job. Check with the Human Resources Department to see if there is a counseling program you can sign up for and whether it is covered under your insurance plan. Asking for help is no longer a stigma, and your employer will see that at least you are trying to change, which could save your job.

Going to Work with a Hangover

There were a lot of Monday mornings where I should have stayed at home. But I always showed up and put in a full day. I know I had to reek of booze.

That's one of the tapes I play in my head if I ever start thinking a beer sounds good. All the way to the Monday morning hangover, where I'm sick enough that normal people would go to the emergency room, and I'd work all day feeling like that. What a way to live!

—Anonymous

If you are so hung over that you feel like calling 911, you shouldn't be going to work, and you are not doing your employer any favors if you show up drunk. Take a personal day instead and go to a doctor, a recovery meeting, or a support group.

Drinking Interfering with Work

Work was that unfortunate interlude that happened between drinking. Got fired, quit, and performed below my capacity—all because of alcohol and other harmful substances.

—Anonymous

If work is something you do to bide your time between boozing, get yourself immediately to a treatment center.

Getting Fired or Quitting Jobs

Lost a job coming in late all the time. Walked out on another one on my own—mainly because it sucked being at work when I was hung over. Does going on an interview, getting the job, then getting drunk and not showing up at all count? I did that a couple of times.

—Anonymous

If you're lucky enough to get a job in this horrible economy, the least you can do is show up—sober.

Drinking at Work

I lost three jobs. I drank in the mornings before work to feel "normal" and to relieve stress. Drank in the bathroom stall at work and later drank on my lunch hour. I was pretty lit by the end of lunch. My one job was balancing the branch cash at the bank. I was the vault teller. I was so hammered, I didn't know up from down.

—Anonymous

I can empathize with this person, because I also drank during my lunch hour and in the mornings to feel "normal." You must try to find a new "normal," one that doesn't involve alcohol—your livelihood depends on it.

Academic Consequences

Crashing academically occurs most often with younger people, who are likely to see their grades slip or are forced to drop out of high school or college because they can't stay sober. It is difficult enough for college-educated women to secure jobs these days; high school dropouts or pregnant teens are robbing themselves of a childhood and the chance for a future with prosperity and personal happiness. If you have to worry about supporting yourself and a child at seventeen, you have catapulted yourself into adulthood with all of its attendant problems and worries. According to the National Institute for Literacy, 85 percent of all juvenile offenders are either functionally or marginally illiterate, and 43 percent of those with poor reading skills are currently living in poverty. As noted earlier, if you continue to drink while pregnant, you are risking the health of your child, who might be born with FASD. Do you really want to be changing diapers or flipping burgers when you could be learning, dating, and enjoying your youth?

My Grade Point Average Fell to a 1.2

Here, twenty-five-year-old Ally, a graduate student, recounts how her grades suffered because of her drinking habit.

I was nine years old the first time I drank to get drunk. My parents weren't alcoholics, but I do have addicts in my family. It wasn't even the first time I drank, but it was the first time I remember drinking to get drunk. It was the Fourth of July, and my parents were having a barbecue. One of my aunts bought me and my two cousins a six-pack of wine coolers.

I remember drinking with my cousins, who were a few years older. I ended up having a whole six-pack of wine coolers and another beer. My little body couldn't handle all that booze, so I got really drunk. My dad kept liquor in the hall closet, and whenever I was home alone, I would sneak alcohol. I remember drinking Southern Comfort right from the bottle without it affecting me. I'd fill the bottle up with water so my parents wouldn't know. Sometimes I would puke in the backyard to try to straighten up.

I stopped drinking for a while and hung out with kids I called the "God Squad" because they went to church all the time. But when I got into high school, I started smoking pot, which I loved. Marijuana became my drug of choice for a while.

I smoked every day, all day long, and drank occasionally. When I was thirteen, I started cutting myself. It would make me feel better somehow. I was trying to feel something and to fill a gap in my life.

When I left home to go to college, I moved in with my high school boyfriend, who was a former drug dealer. He was really jealous and controlling. He hated that I went to school because he thought I was making new friends, but he was the only one I ever talked to. That's when I started drinking again. I felt so lonely and isolated, alcohol became my best friend.

I eventually made a real friend who was in her thirties, and I would go to happy hour and do shots with her and her friends after they finished work. Sometimes I'd stay after they left, long after happy hour ended. Then I'd go home and drink beer and Jack Daniels with my boyfriend. My grades fell to a 1.2 average out of 4.0. I was drinking every day, and really depressed about my life and my horrible relationship. I wasn't doing well in school, so I was depressed about that and wanted to drop out. I lost all my motivation to do anything but go out and drink. My social relationships were more important to me than college. The loneliness and isolation made me continue drinking.

One day I was reading about addiction. I thought if I took classes about this, I'd understand my family better. I never thought of myself as an addict at that time, but as I started taking the classes, I began to recognize things about myself. I broke up with my boyfriend, which I thought would help me stop drinking. My parents got me my own apartment, but I still kept drinking. Every Sunday I'd sit on my porch with a six-pack. I started dating someone else, but my old boyfriend would come to my house and sit outside with a gun. He told me that he wanted to kill himself in front of me so I could see the kind of pain I caused him. It made me feel even more guilt and shame, so I started cutting myself again.

I would get drunk, hook up with a guy for a night, then feel guilty about it and start drinking and cutting myself. I wasn't eating, because I'd lose my appetite whenever I was depressed or stressed. I didn't have a lot of money, so I couldn't afford to buy food *and* buy drinks. Plus, I could get drunk faster on an empty stomach. I lost a lot of weight, of course, and my brother was really worried about me. I spent a few weeks with him, but I'd disappear at night. The courses I was taking on addiction helped get my grades up again. Where I grew up, there weren't any rehabs or AA meetings. Those were for celebrities, we thought, not for regular people like us. Had we known rehabs were available, maybe my friend from high school wouldn't have killed himself trying to get off speed.

Finally, I just got tired of my life. I didn't want to fail out of school. I needed new friends who weren't addicts or alcoholics. One day I walked into a recovery center at school. I felt so alone and embarrassed. I started to leave, but someone stopped me and said that I should stay or at least come back and start hanging out there. I found people my own age who I could talk to and who understood what I was going through. I started going to the recovery center between classes and talking to people. They became my friends, and they are still my friends today.

They encouraged me to go into rehab, which I did, and I started going to AA meetings. I also got medication to help me sleep and alleviate my anxiety. They stopped my desire to drink and to cut myself. I've been sober for three years now, and I'm getting a degree in counseling so I can help other alcoholics get better. There are so many young people like me who suffer alone, but they don't have to. I want to tell them to do what I did, which is to reach out and ask for help.

As you can see from the examples and stories in this chapter, drinking can have a wide variety of negative consequences. Now let's take a look at how to break the cycle and get on the road to recovery.

Part Two

BREAKING THE CYCLE OF ADDICTION

Quiz: The Audit Test*

Take the following quiz if you're wondering whether you or someone you know has had a drinking problem within the last year. Answer the ten questions below honestly (you're the only one who has to see this right now). This quiz could save your life. You can also give this quiz to someone whom you think might have a problem, as a way to open up a conversation about getting help.

Circle the answer that is correct for you:

1. How often do you have a drink containing alcohol?
   a. Never
   b. Once a month or less
   c. 2 to 4 times a month
   d. 2 to 3 times a week
   e. 4 or more times a week

---

* The Audit Test and the Lifetime Test are based on the Alcohol Use Disorders Identification Test (AUDIT) and CAGE tests that appeared in the April 2005 issue of *Alcohol Alert*, published by the U.S. Department of Health and Human Services, the National Institutes of Health, and NIAAA. J. A. Ewing, "Detecting Alcoholism: The CAGE Questionnaire," *Journal of the American Medical Association* 252, no. 14 (1984): 1905–1907; J. B. Saunders, O. G. Aasland, T. F. Babor, et al., "Development of the Alcohol Use Disorders Identification Test (AUDIT): WHO Collaborative Project on Early Detection of Persons with Harmful Alcohol Consumption-II," *Addiction* 88 (1993): 791–804.

2. How many drinks containing alcohol do you have on a typical day when you are drinking?
    a. 1 or 2
    b. 3 or 4
    c. 5 or 6
    d. 7 to 9
    e. 10 or more

3. How often do you have six or more drinks on one occasion?
    a. Never
    b. Less than monthly
    c. Monthly
    d. 2 to 3 times a week
    e. 4 or more times a week

4. How often during the last year have you found that you were not able to stop drinking once you started?
    a. Never
    b. Less than monthly
    c. Monthly
    d. 2 to 3 times a week
    e. 4 or more times a week

5. How often during the last year have you failed to do what was normally expected of you because of drinking?
    a. Never
    b. Less than monthly
    c. Monthly
    d. 2 to 3 times a week
    e. 4 or more times a week

6. How often during the last year have you needed a first drink in the morning to get yourself going after a heavy drinking session?
    a. Never
    b. Less than monthly
    c. Monthly
    d. 2 to 3 times a week
    e. 4 or more times a week

7. How often during the last year have you had a feeling of guilt or remorse after drinking?
   a. Never
   b. Less than monthly
   c. Monthly
   d. 2 to 3 times a week
   e. 4 or more times a week

8. How often during the last year have you been unable to remember what happened the night before because you had been drinking?
   a. Never
   b. Less than monthly
   c. Monthly
   d. 2 to 3 times a week
   e. 4 or more times a week

9. Have you or has someone else been injured as a result of your drinking?
   a. No
   b. Yes, but not in the last year
   c. Yes, during the last year

10. Has a relative or a friend or a doctor or other health-care worker been concerned about your drinking or suggested that you cut down?
    a. No
    b. Yes, but not in the last year
    c. Yes, during the last year

Scoring

For questions 1–8, scores range from 0 to 4
(a = 0; b = 1; c = 2; d = 3; e = 4).

For questions 9–10, scores range from 0 to 4
(a = 0; b = 2; c = 4).

Using the scoring key above, choose the number that corresponds to the answer you selected. Add all of the numbers to obtain your total score. A total score of 8 or higher generally indicates harmful or hazardous drinking behaviors, and you may want to consider seeking help.

Lifetime Drinking Test

Ask yourself the following questions to see whether you might have had a drinking problem during your lifetime.

- Have you felt that you should cut down on your drinking?
- Have people annoyed you by criticizing your drinking?
- Have you ever felt bad or guilty about your drinking?
- Have you ever had a drink first thing in the morning to steady your nerves or to get rid of a hangover?

If you answered yes to two or more of these questions, you have had a drinking problem at some point in your life and should seek professional help (see chapter 6).

9

Choosing Life over Liquor

"Despair comes from trying to control matters over which you have no power. Hope comes from taking responsibility for yourself."

—*Tolbert McCarroll, author and humanitarian*

Resilience

I described all of the various ways to boost your self-esteem, which is an essential step in the coping cycle. Self-esteem will ultimately give you the resilience that's necessary to stay sober. Yet you should always remember the number one reason you can be proud of yourself. It can be the single motivating factor that stops you from having a relapse: you quit drinking. By quitting, you have given up something that you once loved and that once had control over your life. For better or worse, American culture embraces a comeback. You won't see someone on the *Dr. Phil Show* being interviewed because she has been a good wife and mother for thirty years, never broke the law or smoked a cigarette or a joint, or never had a drop of liquor. But if someone comes on declaring that she is twenty days, twenty months, or twenty years sober, chances are the audience will respond with a chorus of applause. Of course, the longer you've been sober, the greater the affirmation, but even at an AA meeting, if you stand up and announce your sobriety, you will hear: "Good for you!" "God bless!" "Way to go!"

People respect those who accomplish their goals, and not drinking is a huge achievement. One reason that recovery groups encourage you to announce your dry date is that it will give you a sense of accomplishment. Even if you slip, you can get a new start date. You've changed your life, and that is no small feat.

I am a big believer in gratitude journals because they remind us about the joys that we often take for granted. Your child's first loose tooth, a good report card, a graduation, losing two pounds, baking a delicious pie, running three miles, or getting a compliment from your boss about how well you handled a difficult situation—these are the joys and triumphs in life that help us get through the triggers and tragedies that pop up like roadblocks to our sobriety.

When my four-year-old grandson put the lid back on a cookie jar, he shouted, "I did it!" with joy and a sense of accomplishment. Women need to own these everyday (or weekly) triumphs, even more than the big stuff. It's not about how attractive we look, how much we weigh, or even how smart we are. If you're facing a hard day at home or at work, coping with the triggers that would otherwise make you want to drink is akin to climbing Mount Everest. You're a genuine success!

Resilience is the ability to bounce back. It's when you are able to say, "I haven't taken a drink today, so the smaller stuff in life really doesn't matter so much." Resilience allows you to make emotional deposits in the bank:

> "I had a terrible argument with my husband, and I didn't take that drink, so I made a deposit in my bank."
>
> "I had a bad day at school today and didn't drink, so I made a deposit in the bank."

Even if you have been in treatment, you are seeing a therapist, or you are going to a support group, your pain won't go away forever. Jobs are going to be lost, people and pets will die, money will be squandered, and relationships will come and go. No one gets a free pass from pain during his or her life. That happens only when we're six feet under.

If you're a woman who drinks too much, the single most important thing you need to develop is the ability to cope with the pains of life without taking a drink. The positive consequences that result once you've stopped drinking will help you build that resilient core. Resilience means being able to get up in the morning, go to work, and be present for your family. It means believing that you can get through life without taking a drink and that you have the strength to bounce back and deal with whatever life throws your way.

For an alcoholic, as difficult as quitting is, it's easy compared to staying sober. If you have been through the wringer of the compulsive cycle, the negative consequences have probably gotten so unbearable that you've finally decided to choose life over liquor. If you've graduated to the coping cycle, you have seen how dramatically your life can change for the better once you learn new ways to deal with your pain, depression, or anxiety. Or maybe, as the AA saying goes, you simply got sick and tired of being sick and tired. Whatever brought you to this place—be it a husband or a partner who threatened to leave, a friend or a family member who begged you to stop, a boss who warned you that your job is on the line, or a befuddled child who asked, "Mommy, why do you drink so much?"—you are on your way to ending the spin cycle of insanity.

It doesn't matter why or how you got to this point, the fact that you have decided to stop drinking is a remarkable achievement for which you should be proud. You are on your way to becoming your "best self," and I promise that should you stay the course, your very worst day of your new life will be better than your very best day of drinking!

The Most Common Excuses for Not Quitting

Part of staying sober is letting go of your stubborn denial about your alcoholism. In the many years that I have been a recovery specialist and counselor, I have heard just about every excuse imaginable for why people don't want to stop drinking. Many of these excuses have become clichés within the community of alcoholics, and they are red flags that you are not ready to jump off the compulsive merry-go-round.

For those of you who have not yet made that decision to stop, I offer the following oft-used justifications for why you think you should continue to drink. If any of these sound familiar, go back to the beginning of this book and reread it. You might not be ready to stop now, but I have faith that you will get there someday soon.

- I can quit any time I want to.

    This kind of self-denial stems from the belief that you are in total control of your behavior and that you will stop drinking once you make up your mind to do so. The truth is, you simply don't *want* to stop. Unfortunately, this kind of alcoholic rarely makes the decision to stop drinking on her own. If you think you can stop any time, I have a challenge for you: try going a day, a week, or a month without any booze, and see what happens.

- I'm not doing anything illegal.

    Well, true, unless you're under twenty-one or driving while drunk. Cigarettes are also legal, don't forget, but that doesn't mean they won't give you cancer if you smoke enough of them! It's also legal in many states to carry a handgun, but consuming too much alcohol is like taking that pistol and playing Russian roulette. You never know which drink is going to be the one that kills you.

- My drinking is not that bad.

    If this sounds familiar, you have an inkling that you might have a drinking problem, but, in your estimation, it hasn't really gotten out of control—yet. You resolutely maintain even in the face of increasing evidence to the contrary that your drinking is not really as bad as others make it out to be. You honestly don't understand what people are talking about when they say you have a drinking problem, and you are deeply offended by the suggestion that you might be an alcoholic. You react with anger, resentment and, of course, more drinking when people suggest that you have a problem. One of the most meaningful comments my counselor gave me while I was in treatment was, "You haven't lost control *yet, but* it's coming—it always comes!"

- I'm just having fun!

    Social drinkers do have fun because, as I wrote earlier, alcohol often makes them feel better, which is why they do it so often. Yet there are other, safer ways to have fun, many of which I've included in this book. We all want to have a good time but not at the expense of our health, emotional well-being, and the people around us.

- If you were me, you'd drink, too.

    This drinker is the kind who likes to throw herself a good old-fashioned pity party. As I've said, we all have troubles and pain in our lives, but the depressed drunk feels victimized, is often resentful and sullen, and is convinced that everyone and everything is against her. Her unhappiness gives her the license to act up by saying "bottom's up." She believes that drinking is her only solace, in what she sees as a cruel, heartless world.

- Drinking makes me funnier/sexier/more interesting/more confident.

    Alcohol unleashes our inhibitions, which allows us to speak more freely and candidly in social situations. For some women, especially barhoppers who are unsure about their attractiveness, alcohol also acts as an ego booster, allowing them to feel more comfortable with dating and socializing. The same goes, however, for shy women at parties, in business meetings, or simply when being introduced to new people. Having a shot gives them the confidence that they otherwise lack.

    The trick for those in need of booster shots is to discover your real self-confidence without the help of mind-altering substances. If you're witty, attractive, interesting, and poised when you're tipsy, you have the ability to summon those parts of yourself when you are sober. It's still you, right? The person talking, flirting, or holding court at a dinner party isn't an imposter. Don't let alcohol be your Cyrano. Do some practice runs socializing without the booze to see whether you can lose your insecurity without an ice-clinking crutch in your hand.

- I'm just doing what everyone else does.

How many mothers have heard this battle cry from their children about why they should be allowed to (fill in the blank) because every one else on the planet is doing it, and they're the only ones who are being put in a moralistic prison. This excuse is used most often by younger alcoholics when explaining to parents why that keg party where they passed out and had to be carried home was simply a rite of passage that all of the kids engage in.

It's no secret that alcohol is being consumed in high schools and colleges across the country, but "everyone" does not have to include your teenager or coed. There are people who choose not to drink until their twenty-first birthday or to limit themselves to one or two drinks, even when they go out to a bar or to parties. It's called judgment and maturity, and the age-old maternal edict "If everyone jumped off the bridge, would you do it, too?" applies to alcohol as well.

- I can handle my liquor.

Really? So you're one of those hollow-legged alcoholics who can drink everyone under table. Let's say this is true. If so, it means your body has learned to tolerate enormous quantities of alcohol, which, as I explained in earlier chapters, is wreaking havoc on your internal organs and is even more of a reason to stop immediately. If you no longer get a buzz when you drink and you are simply "maintaining," you are even more far gone than you realize.

- I'm not hurting anybody but myself!

First, this is blatantly not true, because alcoholics hurt everyone they come in contact with, including family, friends, coworkers, you name it. Second, if you truly believe what you say, do you care so little about yourself that you think it's okay to self-destruct?

- You knew I liked to drink when you met me.

   There's a difference between enjoying a cocktail or fine wine once in a while and being a raging alcoholic. Alcoholism can be a gradual descent into the dark side, so just because you knew someone liked to drink when you first met him or her doesn't mean you have to accept that your friend, spouse, or family member has a debilitating addiction.

- I have to drink for my work!

   I talked about this in my section on barhopping. Some women are in professions where they must wine and dine clients, and drinking is often involved. Account executives, public relations reps, and salespeople are often expected to go to parties and events as part of their jobs, but just because your coworkers or colleagues are doing shots doesn't mean you can't call the shots when it comes to what is in *your* glass.

   Show your clients a good time by taking them to a four-star restaurant, instead of to a bar, or to a sporting event or a play, instead of to a club. If your guests want to drink, ask for a seltzer and lime so that you can keep your sobriety and wits intact. If someone asks why you're not drinking, simply say that you are the designated driver or you are taking a medication and can't drink. In the majority of cases, drinking in work situations will negatively affect your performance, and you might end up doing or saying something you regret when you are entertaining under the influence.

- You're no angel, either!

   Sometimes the best defense is a good offense, so an alcoholic might recite a laundry list of your bad habits to give herself permission to misbehave. Simply admit that you are not perfect, but at least you don't pass out in your dinner plate. Drunks can be mean when they are toasted, so don't take it personally when they lash out. At the same time, don't let them cow you into accepting their unacceptable behavior. Instead, offer to get help for your problem if they agree to get help for theirs.

- I'll quit tomorrow.

  Thank you, Scarlett O'Hara. For those readers old enough to recognize this reference, it is from *Gone with the Wind*, where Southern belle and heroine Scarlet stared adversity in the face (for example, the burning of Atlanta during the Civil War), with the charmingly dismissive phrase, "I'll think about it tomorrow." Unfortunately, if the alcoholic is waiting until she gets through some difficult period in her life before she decides to quit drinking, there will inevitably be another trying situation that pulls up to the curbside, forcing her to go on another alcoholic joy ride.

  The best response for the Scarlett O'Hara drinker is: "I know you are going through a hard time, but there is no time like the present to start your recovery. Booze is not going to make the situation any better. Chances are, it will only make things worse." You might also want to ask, "How, exactly, will tomorrow be any different from today unless you stop drinking?"

- Nobody is going to tell me what to do!

  "Give me martinis or give me death!" is the battle cry of this teed-off party girl. Be careful what you wish for, because, unfortunately, you might get both if you drink enough Cosmos. These stubborn drinkers are like rubber bands that snap back if you try to pull them hard enough in the direction of sobriety. It's best to wait for these alcoholics to make it their decision to stop drinking.

- I'd be okay if it weren't for (fill in the blank).

  These alcoholics like to blame others for their drinking. If it weren't for (their jobs, their husbands, their kids, their parents, whatever), they'd be as sober as a judge. It's a lot easier to blame others for their behavior than to take responsibility for their own actions. If this sounds like you, the first thing you must do is woman up and stop pointing fingers at others for the problems in your life.

- I'll handle it myself!

   In this case, the alcoholic fully acknowledges that she has a problem but is adamant that she can sober up without any kind of professional help or support group. This pull-yourself-up-by-your-own-booze-straps alcoholic believes that getting off the juice is simply a matter of willpower. If you believe this to be true, you must remember that a physical withdrawal occurs when the toxic chemicals that you've been pouring into your body no longer take control of your brain. Aside from the emotional connection you have to booze, your body now craves this substance, which I will talk about at greater length later. Detoxing isn't pretty and often requires medical attention, so the more people you have in your corner, the better your chances of getting and staying sober.

SOBERING THOUGHTS

The following is a post from 43things.com, an online goal-setting community.

"Well, today is day 19 and I almost slipped up a couple days ago. It was day 16 and cracked open a beer and stared at it for like two minutes. But then I poured it out and drank a Diet Coke. I can't believe I've made it to 19 days so far. I haven't been this sober for this long since high school. My birthday is this Monday, so that one will be tough too but I'm still not gonna drink. I gonna make it to 30 days!"

10

Recovery Strategies

The first step in your recovery process is finding a way to stop the knee-jerk (some might say elbow-jerk) reaction to reach for a drink whenever you're faced with the hard knocks of life. As I established in part one, the factors that keep you circling the drain of addiction are everyday stress, feeling stigmatized by alcoholism, and your past or present pain. The second part of this book is about developing new ways to cope with pain.

Unlike the compulsive cycle that keeps you stuck in the vortex of alcoholism, the coping cycle will allow you to transition to the recovery stage. It's important to remember that alcoholism is not about the booze—it's about how you choose to deal with the stress in your life. The bottle is only one symptom of what is really going on. In other words, if you stop drinking, you are not necessarily in recovery. You could be what is commonly known among twelve-steppers as a "dry drunk." Unless you either follow whatever program you are in or face up to your inner demons, you are just one beer/vodka/(insert your poison) away from a relapse. Once you find a way to cope with your pain (and I will discuss various ideas in this chapter), you will develop the resiliency you need never to drink again. The coping cycle looks like this:

Pain

↓

Coping

↓

Self-Esteem

↓

Positive Consequences

↓

Resiliency

Whatever support system you choose, it should fit your particular lifestyle. The following recommendations are tailored to the type of alcoholic you are. Just because someone else white-knuckled her way to recovery or another person stopped drinking by reconnecting with her religion, that doesn't mean those will work for you. Recovery is not one-size-fits-all. As I established, everyone has a different source of pain and is in a different stage of life. A teenage girl who was sexually abused by her priest might not feel comfortable going to a church meeting. Likewise, an overweight woman might not want to take a yoga class in order to get healthier and meet new friends.

Once you choose the lifestyle change or activity that is right for you and that really addresses the pain that you have lived with for so long, the desire to self-medicate will decrease and, hopefully, disappear entirely. When that happens, the negative consequences you once experienced when you were in the throes of the disease will be replaced by positive ones. The more self-esteem you develop, the more resilient you will be to the temptations of drinking and the pain that we all experience during our lives. I realize that nothing about recovery is easy. "One day at a time" is not a cliché, it's a credo. So, here are some steps women need to take in order to cope with their pain—whether they are teenagers, millennials, boomers, or seniors.

Tell Someone

Alcoholics Anonymous has a system in which members are required to find a "sponsor." This is someone you can call, e-mail, or text, day or night, whenever you feel the urge to drink. Because many women are ashamed of their drinking, they are reluctant to share their stories with others, but this is an essential step in the recovery process. Find someone whom you trust, preferably not a family member, a love interest, or a drinking buddy (unless he or she has decided to join you in recovery). When there are hurt feelings caused by the alcoholic's past behavior, your guilt and shame can resurface, which can sabotage the coping cycle. Because family members can sometimes act as "enablers" (unconsciously encouraging your drinking), unless they've gone to Al-Anon or another therapy for family and friends of alcoholics, they could do more harm than good. Calling a person who shares or understands your problem, even if she's a stranger, is better than depending on someone you are related to or intimate with. Call her what you want—sponsor, friend, mentor, counselor, or sober sister—you need someone to put on speed dial.

Make New Friends

In addition to finding a sponsor or a mentor, you should find new friends whom you did not socialize with when you were drinking. These new friends will act as a support group during the good and the bad times. For alcoholic women, it is especially important to have girlfriends who will circle their wagons whenever you are in danger of falling off yours. This might mean finding new friends for whom alcohol is not the center of their universe.

There are now women-only recovery groups, where you may feel more comfortable opening up about your drinking and the issues that led to you becoming an alcoholic. You can also find activities such as charities, sewing circles, yoga, bible studies, bridge clubs, cooking classes, sports teams, or book groups where women are engaged in something they are passionate about and where no wine or liquor is served. Once you reach a certain point in your sobriety, you will be able to gather together with people who drink, and you won't be tempted. Yet in the beginning, it is wise to be completely dry. Socializing with new friends and engaging in new activities will help you make a lifestyle change, especially when you do this regularly.

You can also design your own support network (pick an activity of choice), but it's important to have a buddy or two who will encourage you to stick to the program. If you're a closet drinker who spends a lot of time drinking alone, as I did, simply finding a reason to get out of the house can be a step in the right direction (I will talk more about that later). For barhoppers, finding a social circle that doesn't involve drinking for entertainment (good-bye, karaoke bar) will be the challenge, and for women who are depressed, discovering something that will give them the emotional stimulation they crave will produce the best and most positive results.

If you want to keep the friends you have, tell them that you are trying to stop drinking and that you are not judging them or telling them what *they* should do. Let them know that you love them and that they are welcome to join you in your quest for sobriety. If they refuse, tell them you understand, wish them luck, and let them go.

Trigger Points

All alcoholics have triggers points that can bring on a relapse. There are three common trigger points that often drive people to drink, and every alcoholic has at least one. The first is a crisis, such as a death, an illness, a financial downturn, or other tragic events. The second and perhaps most common trigger point for women has to do with relationships, which includes break-ups, divorces, family squabbles, spousal abuse, or friendships gone sour. I've known women in recovery who were in unhappy relationships for years, but once they got separated or divorced, they relapsed.

The third trigger point, especially for women, has to do with holidays or events that evoke an emotional response. These can be birthdays, graduations, weddings, births, reunions, anniversaries, Christmas, Thanksgiving, Independence Day, and, the biggest one for drinkers, New Year's Eve.

There are more trigger points, of course, that can set a woman off. Again, they can vary, depending on your age and situation. A nasty comment from a boss, a friend, a frenemy, or a family member can spark a relapse. A trigger could even be a childhood memory that resurfaces from time to time, despite your best efforts to repress it. Talking to a therapist, a sponsor, or a mentor about your trigger points can help you keep them in control. You can start by making a list of your triggers and carrying it with you, along with your favorite affirmations, so that you will be prepared for certain volatile situations. Doing a relaxation technique might also help calm you down during a trigger episode. Triggers can spring up any time or anywhere, whether it's at the end of the day; before, during, or after work; while you're taking care of the kids; or while you're watching TV and contemplating your life. Here are some other ways to deal with your personal triggers:

Trigger people. As I mentioned earlier, hanging out with bar buddies or other barflies will encourage you to drink. If your friends say things like, "Oh, come on, you're not an alcoholic!" or, "Have another one with me," tell them that you are no longer drinking, and that it is difficult for you to see them. If simply talking to them makes you thirsty, you must cut them off completely and let the voice mail pick up when they call, or you might even need to change your number. The same goes for abusive husbands or boyfriends. Either try to work it out in couple's counseling or get out of the relationship! If you are in physical danger, find a shelter where you and your children will be safe.

Trigger places. Avoid going to bars, restaurants, or the homes of people where you drank in the past. Pretend that these buildings have been condemned, if the image helps you point your compass in another direction. This might mean avoiding your high school or college reunion until you are sure that you won't relapse at the sight of the campus pub. Find new places to go out with your friends, where everyone (including the bartender) doesn't know your name.

Trigger things. Objects can also trigger a drinking response, such as cigarettes (if you always drink and smoke) or pictures of your old boyfriends, ex-husbands, estranged family members, or wild vacations. Put them away in an attic or a basement, or throw them out so that they won't come back to haunt you. Pawn or give away the engagement ring that reminds you of a divorce or a break-up. The act of clearing out bad memories can be liberating, but you don't have to throw these keepsakes away if you don't want to—if you are the sentimental type, give them to a friend or a family member to store for you until you have the willpower to face them without the fear of relapse.

Be Honest

By the time you're an alcoholic, dishonesty has become second nature to you. You often lie about your liquor consumption and about the consequences of your drunken behavior. You hide and lie about the fact that you've relapsed. After a while, you get so good at lying to others that you end up lying to yourself. The problem with lying, other than making you feel guilty and ashamed, is that lying makes it difficult for you to like yourself, which is an essential part of the coping and recovery cycles. The more you lie, the less you like yourself, which makes you want to drink again and continue to lie. Lying will throw you right back into the twister of compulsive behavior.

If you are an alcoholic woman, one of the important steps to recovery is being honest with yourself about your addiction. AA calls it "rigorous honesty." It's not some half-baked, partial truth—it's a slap in the face, a look-at-yourself-clearly-in-the-mirror type of truth. It's the ability to be honest with yourself, despite the consequences. Here's how Mary (fourteen years clean) explained her experience with rigorous honesty on her blog *Being Sober*:

> I remember when I was in my first year of sobriety, I worked at a large insurance brokerage firm with mostly lawyers. I had to call a lawyer one afternoon and tell him that I made a huge mistake on his policy, and it had pretty serious consequences for him. He told me that he appreciated my honesty, but "What the hell was I going to do about it?" He was not nice. I went to an AA meeting that night and told my group that this "rigorous honesty" crap was a bunch of nonsense. It didn't work in the real world. You couldn't go around admitting you were wrong in business—especially with lawyers!
>
> I got the problem with his account worked out in the next week. And about a week later, the CEO of the company brought me a copy of a letter the lawyer had written about how wonderful I was! He said he appreciated my honesty and my work to get my error straightened out! I took the letter, reduced it to the size of a business card, and had it laminated. I put it in my wallet and carried that thing around with me for years as a reminder that rigorous honesty does work in the real world!

As Mary's experience illustrates, the price of dishonesty is too high for alcoholics. Because it's not about how much you drink (most drunks know exactly how much they need to get through a day or a night), it's about understanding and revealing the consequences of your drinking. Telling yourself, "It wasn't so bad," is a flat-out lie. It's *that* bad, my tipsy friend; in fact, it's probably worse than you think.

The other thing you must be honest about is how other people perceive you. You might tell yourself you're normal, especially if you are a "functional alcoholic," but ask some people who *really* know you, and you might be surprised by their answers.

Recovery requires complete honesty. It requires being absolutely honest with the people who support you: your family, your doctor, your therapist, your 12-step group, your sober sisters, or your mentor. If you can't be completely honest with them, you can't be honest with yourself. When you lie, you are leaving the door open to relapse.

I realize that honesty won't come easily in the beginning—it certainly didn't for me! You've spent so much time learning how to lie that telling the truth, no matter how important it is for your recovery, will feel strange. It's like learning a new language. You might have to practice telling the truth over and over again before you are fluent. When you first start, you might even have to stop yourself in mid-lie. If this happens, don't worry about the embarrassment. Just suck it up and say, "You know what? That's not exactly the way it happened." I promise that you'll feel so much better if you do this.

Believe Your Life Can Be Different

Ask yourself, will more lying, isolation, and drinking make you happier? If your answer is yes, you might as well put this book down and go mix yourself a cocktail. If not, it's time to create a new life for yourself. Here's another sobering thought for those of you who have a family history of alcoholism. A new study suggests that the key to long-term happiness has a lot to do with the choices we make in life.

Based on a twenty-five-year German study of more than sixty thousand participants, scientists may be moving beyond their earlier "set point theory" of happiness. According to that theory, 50 percent of the population had a "set point" for happiness, which seemed to be based on genetics and early childhood experiences. These people tended to stay at the same level of happiness and satisfaction during their entire lives. The other 50 percent of the population were thought to experience changes in life satisfaction over time, but one-third of the changes were negative, based on events such as the death of a spouse, and two-thirds were positive but small changes. The set point theory stated that it's easy for us to become unhappy over negative life events, but harder to become happier by making better choices. These conclusions, however, seem to be disproved by the recently announced results of the long-term German study. Scientists were excited to discover that choices we make *do* have a major impact on our life satisfaction and how happy we are. A key factor is what we choose to prioritize in life. People who give more importance to relationships, family, and meaningful work are happier than those who put achievement and material gain in first place. It seems that how we relate to our partners, how we balance our lives between work and leisure time, how and with whom we choose to socialize, and whether we decide to follow a healthful lifestyle are key factors in determining our life satisfaction.

In other words, biology is not necessarily your destiny. Whether you learn it from a mentor, a sponsor, a pastor, or a power greater than yourself that comes from above or from within, you must believe that you can and will change your life. Think of it this way: you might be an alcoholic now, but you have an opportunity to live another way. Changing your life might be difficult, but it can also be incredibly rewarding.

Recovery gives you a sense of accomplishment, even if that accomplishment consists of not drinking for twenty-four hours. This is no small achievement, and it's one that you can be proud of! Imagine how you will feel once you cross the twenty-four-hour mark! Think about how you will feel once you've stayed sober for a month. Recovery means you get a second chance. Some people aren't fortunate enough to get that, and I personally know people who didn't give themselves that second chance at happiness. Some people are satisfied simply to exist, no matter how awful that might be.

People in recovery sometimes describe themselves as "grateful" addicts. I know that I give thanks for my recovery every day. Why would an alcoholic be grateful? Because recovering from an addiction can help you find an inner peace that you never felt before and that many people never get the opportunity to experience.

Get Off the Elevator

We know that alcoholism is a disease, but at some point you must take responsibility for how you live with your illness. For certain people, it takes hitting the bottom; others are able to stop before they crash and burn (literally, if they are drunk behind the wheel of a car). Dr. Tom, the former priest who helped Cheryl with her recovery, likes to use the following analogy. "Alcoholism," he says, "is like an elevator that goes in only one direction—down. You can choose what floor you want to get off. Every alcoholic gets off at a different floor, and some go in and out of the elevator for years, but the main thing is that you stop the descent before you hit the basement."

What Dr. Tom is saying is that recovery can't happen unless you get off that elevator. The people who fail are the ones who believe that they can't face their husbands or their jobs or their friends without another drink. They do not believe in their hearts that they are capable of stepping through those open doors into the freedom of sobriety. Of course, there will always be the lost causes, but the core of the recovery process is that you won't gain the self-respect you need to stay sober unless you understand that you are destroying your life or your family's life.

What makes the Core Recovery Process model different from others is that it recognizes that you won't stop drinking by having someone else tell you that you're a drunken loser. Instead, you need to tell yourself that you are going to triumph in your battle with addiction. It might not happen today, and it might not even happen tomorrow, but someday you will find the strength to do it.

Calling It Quits

If you have finally come to grips with the fact that you are a raging alcoholic (or even a whimpering one), the first thing you must do is stop drinking. I know that sounds as if I'm asking you to levitate, but you can do it!

Start by resolving that today will be the day you will not take another drink. Remember, it is very important to check with your

physician before going "cold turkey" by yourself. Most detox experiences from alcohol need to be medically supervised. Also, let
someone whom you trust know about your decision so that you
will have a cheerleader, as well as a lifeguard, by your side. Don't
ask yourself to do any more than that—for now. Take it, as they say,
one day at a time. Later I'll suggest some ways to stay on the wagon
that worked for the alcoholic women I've known or counseled.

A GLOSSARY OF TREATMENT TERMS

Before I get into the nitty-gritty of staying sober, I want you to
understand the terminology used by women who drink too
much and those who help them.

Detox:

Short for "detoxification," when you check into a medical facility for help in getting yourself off the alcohol, you are going
through detox, which usually takes place during the first two
to five days of abstinence. Detox can be done in a hospital, at
a detox center, or at an alcohol treatment facility. It does not
necessarily go hand in hand with psychological counseling.

Inpatient:

Inpatient treatment means you are required to stay at a facility, such as a hospital or a rehab center. Another term for this
is "residential" treatment.

Interventions:

This is when family, friends, colleagues, clergy, and counselors all join forces to confront your drinking problem. An intervention is a bit like a surprise party with no spiked punch,
where the guest of honor is told exactly how she has negatively affected her loved ones as a result of her drinking. The
husband might say, "You passed out and left our kids unat-
tended," and a friend might say, "I love you, but you are a
mean drunk, and I can't be with you when you are hammered,
which has been almost every time I see you."

One young woman came to see me before her mother's
intervention. She had grown up with an alcoholic mother, so
the happiest memory she had was of going away to college.
When I asked her what she was going to say to her mother,

she said, "Mom, you forgot my birthday yesterday, and it made me feel as if you didn't love me."

In other words, everyone gets to air a laundry list of grievances and actual behaviors that have been witnessed, in the hope that it will motivate and encourage the alcoholic to stop drinking. Although group interventions work by addressing the denial, they can also backfire by sending the alcoholic into a free-fall, due to guilt and shame. The most successful interventions usually have strong therapists who lead the group so that it doesn't turn into an emotional stoning.

Outpatient:

Outpatient services are when you see a doctor but do not have to pack a suitcase. If you are working, you can continue to do so while getting treatment. Services include seeing a private counselor once a week for an hour or attending a group led by a trained professional each week. There is also intensive outpatient treatment, which involves counseling three or four days a week, often for more than an hour at a clip. It can be done in the mornings or the evenings.

Partial Care:

For those who need even more intensive treatment, you can see an individual counselor or have group therapy and alcohol education for up to six hours a day, four or five days a week.

Rehab:

Short for "rehabilitation," rehab might include detox, medical treatment, counseling, or a combination of all three.

Treatment:

When those of us in the recovery business talk about treatment, we are usually referring to a combination of therapy (group or individual), educational services, and family or peer group support.

What to Expect

The Physical Fallout

Although some people can quit cold turkey, this can be medically risky, depending on how much you used to drink. Your mind might be willing, but your body is not, so you need to know what to expect when you go into withdrawal. An alcoholic's body is like a newborn baby who needs the bottle every two to four hours. Your body demands the alcohol and eagerly awaits it. If you stop suddenly, your body will react, sometimes violently, to the craving. Because alcohol depresses the central nervous system, which slows down your heart, lungs, and other basic functions, your system will speed up when it is not given alcohol. This biological reaction to withdrawal can cause a spike in blood pressure or even renal (kidney) failure, which can be life threatening. It can take your body between two and five days to adjust to being "dry"—even longer if you were a heavy drinker.

The made-for-TV version of withdrawal might show a heaving, shaky, and sweaty drunk. Unfortunately, this scenario is closer to menopause than it is to alcohol withdrawal. *The Lost Weekend* version includes the shakes, headaches, sleeplessness, flop sweats, confusion, visual and auditory hallucinations (aka the "DTs"), anxiety, vomiting, high blood pressure, and seizures. Kicking alcohol is actually more dangerous than withdrawing from drugs such as meth or cocaine. For some people, the physical symptoms last only a few days; for others, they can last a week or up to ten days. Keep in mind that the experience of withdrawal varies for each individual.

This is why you *must* consult with your physician or go to a local treatment center to see whether detoxing from alcohol will cause you any immediate harm. I cannot emphasize enough the importance of seeking medical supervision as you begin this journey to sobriety. Serious withdrawal symptoms can be treated with medication, such as benzodiazepines, which must be prescribed by a doctor. If you already have a physician, be honest with him or her about your alcohol use. I realize this can be difficult for many women who are ashamed of their addiction, but alcoholism is a disease, and you wouldn't be afraid to talk to your doctor if you had cancer, would you? It might be easier if you start by saying that you are an alcoholic, but you intend to quit drinking. Believe me, you will get kudos, not dirty stares, for this. Your doctor can then design a plan of action for getting you through the first few days of withdrawal and can help you with your symptoms. If you don't have a doctor, you can admit yourself into a detox center, a hospital, or an alcohol treatment facility that has a detox unit. Medical professionals who are familiar with alcohol and drug withdrawals will be able to guide you through this process, check your vital signs, and give you medication, if necessary, to control your symptoms. Again, do not try to white-knuckle your detox by yourself. There are so many places to go for help; you should not have to go it alone.

Once you have taken care of the medical issues, it is important to decide exactly how you want to approach staying sober. Treatment centers can be costly. If you have health insurance, you might find that it covers some, if not all, of your treatment. Check with your provider to see whether there are centers "in network" before you look at outside alternatives. Make sure to ask how much is covered, whether there are copays or deductibles, the time limits for follow-up services, and whether your employer must be notified.

If you are not insured, many state-supported agencies are not as expensive as the private facilities or rehabs that the rich and famous check into. Some government-funded programs work on a sliding-scale fee basis, which depends on your income. Some states even offer free or reduced-cost treatment, so find out how you can apply for this, if you have low or no income. If you are on Medicaid, then you might be able to find facilities that will waive the cost of services. I suggest locating a treatment center that fits your needs, as well as your budget. If you have young children, you must also consider who will be looking after them while you are away.

The Emotional Fallout

Aside from the physical reactions that you will experience after quitting, you will likely suffer emotional fallout that can manifest in myriad ways. Some women might feel depressed, as if their best friend suddenly died or moved away. Others might feel angry, jittery, anxious, or even terrified. These emotions can come in waves and may be overwhelming at times.

One reason for this newfound rush of emotion is that alcohol once suppressed many of these feelings. As I explained about pain in chapter 2, heavy drinking has a numbing effect, both physically and emotionally, which is why it was sometimes used in the battle-field if an anesthetic wasn't available. The very reason many people become alcoholics in the first place was that it enabled them to put their emotions into a deep freeze. Once you stop drinking, you will no longer be able to ignore these raw emotions and feelings, so they will rise to the surface, where your new sober self must deal with them. Whatever you do, don't be tempted to start drinking again just because you feel sad, angry, or uncomfortable.

This is when talking to a mental health professional can be helpful. Don't keep these feelings locked up inside yourself—let someone know what is going on. Remind yourself that these disturbing emotions will settle down the longer you are sober, and you will eventually be on an even keel. The time it takes for this to happen varies with each individual. Again, look for ways to distract yourself from your moodiness. Talk to someone and give yourself a pep talk by saying that you can and will get through this period of early sobriety. You've gone through so much up until now, why stop here?

Find safe and healthy ways to express and experience your feelings. If you feel like crying, go ahead and have a good cry. Rent the saddest movie you know and watch it with a box of tissues nearby. The sheer act of releasing your emotions and tears might make you feel better. Writing your feelings down in a journal or on a blog might also help you let these feelings go. This is where women have an advantage over men, because there is no social taboo against women expressing our sadness or weaknesses.

Coping Skills for Women Who Drink Too Much

We all must find our own way to cope with the pain that we are experiencing, depending on our age and stage of life. Once that occurs in your life, the positive consequences will replace the negative ones that had buried your hopes and dreams. You will regain your self-esteem by building a new foundation that is resilient enough to endure the dips that life brings your way so that you can have a lifetime of recovery. The following tips have helped me cope with the stress in my life and are worth trying, even if the new activities take a few weeks or longer to become a part of your everyday routine.

Learn to Relax

Women use alcohol as a means to escape and reward themselves. If you lead a stressful life (and who doesn't?), then you need to change whatever creates tension in your life. Anxiety, depression, and the inability to relax are among the most common causes of relapse. It is essential that you learn new ways to relax if you want to acquire the coping skills you need for a happier, sober life. It will be difficult at first, because alcoholics don't know how to relax without drinking. For some people, it's been their only means of escape.

I have treated thousands of patients, many of whom told me that learning new ways to relax has changed their lives. There is only one reason (other than being an addict) that people don't relax—they think they're too busy to slow down. It goes something like this: "I want to relax, but I've got to go shopping for dinner, clean the house, pick up the kids, get that project done at work, buy that birthday present for my mother . . ." and so on, and so on. Now ask yourself how much time you spend drinking. If you add up all of the time it takes to buy your liquor, use it, hide it, deal with the consequences, and plan your next relapse, you'll find the time to do something else so that you can take a breather.

Learning to relax without drinking is not optional—it is crucial to your recovery. Start by going one hour or one day (depending on your problem) without drinking and substituting another activity during the time that you would otherwise be drinking. It could be going to an AA meeting, talking to a therapist or your mentor, or using one of the numerous relaxation techniques that have been proved to change our brains, as well as our bodies. It can range from going for a walk in the park or the woods to more structured forms of relaxation, such as meditation, yoga, or running. If you're under a lot of stress, you might ask a doctor to prescribe an appropriate antianxiety medication. Be careful, though, and make sure that your physician knows about your alcohol issues—prescription drugs are usually not the answer. Use any of these techniques or a combination of them, but do something every day to relax, escape, reward yourself, and turn off the chatter in your mind.

It's harder for teens to relax, because their lives are so frenetic, but they can channel that energy into other activities that don't involve partying with alcohol. Adolescents should think about their favorite (sober) ways to unwind: talking on the phone to a friend, playing soccer or volleyball or being on a gymnastics team, reading an absorbing book, writing in a journal, drawing, or even playing video games, which can be addictive in another way but it's better than using drugs or alcohol.

Dean Ornish, M.D., who writes about preventing heart disease, wrote a book called *The Spectrum*, which devotes an entire chapter to breathing and meditation. Dr. Andrew Weil also writes about the importance of breathing and guided meditation. Anyone at any age can use Dr. Herbert Benson's relaxation response when she is feeling stressed out.

He developed the relaxation response at Harvard, and it has been scientifically proved to relieve tension, especially if used on a regular basis. It can be done while you exercise or engage in other activities. His book of the same name will explain more about how to use the techniques, but you'll need to remember only these two steps to elicit the relaxation response:

1. The repetition of a word, a sound, a prayer, or a muscular activity.
2. When everyday thoughts intrude, return to a passive repetition of this word, phrase, or sound. As I said, this can be done during yoga, tai chi, a repetitive prayer, such as the rosary, meditation, or a repetitive physical exercise such as running.

Practicing the relaxation response will help reverse or prevent the stress that causes you to drink. Because our brains are constantly running, one of hardest parts of the relaxation response is learning how to control our thoughts and focus our minds on a single word, phrase, or sound and our breathing. Clearing your mind is like emptying the recycle bin of old files on your computer or taking the clutter out of an overstuffed drawer. It's a cleansing process that makes us feel better in the end. Like any new skill, it takes practice, but don't give up.

Ultimately, it doesn't matter how many times you practice the relaxation response, as long as you do regularly. The more you use it, the more effective it becomes, and the more you will feel the difference. As Dr. Benson's research shows, the relaxation response can be achieved by repetitive prayer, such as reciting the rosary, chanting, or doing focused breathing. It's about quieting your mind and finding a place of inner peace and joy. Over time, you will find that you can use this technique whenever you feel anxious or have the urge to drink.

Eat Right and Be Merry

A crucial part of learning new ways to cope with your anxiety involves taking better care of yourself nutritionally. You can do this by being aware of what you eat (and drink). Now that the toxins have left your body, you should try to eat well-balanced, nutritionally rich meals and drink healthy beverages. Remember the old Food Pyramid that we used to follow? The latest 2010 Dietary Guidelines from the U.S. Department of Agriculture have done away with that geometric diagram and call for Americans to focus instead on balancing calories with physical activity, as well as eating more healthy foods, such as vegetables, fruits, whole grains, fat-free and low-fat dairy products, and seafood. It is also important to cut down on sodium (salt), saturated and trans fats, sugars, and refined grains.

Simply put, the USDA advises us to enjoy our food but to eat less (no all-you-can-stuff buffets).

Avoid oversize portions. (I actually use smaller plates, which helps me control my portion size. Another trick is never to serve anything larger than your fist.)

Fill half of your plate with fruits and vegetables.

Switch to fat-free or low-fat (1%) milk.

Read labels for calorie counts and the amount of sodium in your soup, bread, and frozen meals.

No sugary soda or over-caffeinated drinks, please. I realize that any soda is better than alcohol, and if you must have a vice, it's not the worst one, but why drink your calories? Studies have shown that soft drinks, even diet ones, are the main source of weight gain for Americans, so stick with a nice refreshing glass of water. You don't have to buy bottled, either, if you live in a town or a city that has a good water system (plus, you don't want to add to the plastic waste disposal problem). Using water filters is another way to get rid of any foul-tasting mineral deposits in your local water.

Avoid processed and refined foods and anything that you can buy at a drive-through or that has more than five unpronounceable ingredients. Many prepared food products that you find in the supermarket have added sugar; for example, white breads, sweetened cereal, cooks, crackers, chips, candy, white potatoes, and white rice. Opt for whole grain and brown rice instead. Whole-grain or whole-wheat flour is a better option than white flour when baking. If sugar (or its cousins, fructose, cane juice, corn syrup, sucrose, and glucose) are listed in the first three ingredients, put the food item back on the shelf.

Share mealtime with others, such as friends and family, so that eating becomes an enjoyable social ritual, rather than a habitual chore. I especially like to join hands with people around our table and give thanks. Even if you're alone, filling your heart with gratitude is a perfect way to begin each meal.

The more colorful your meals, the healthier your diet. I'm not talking about food coloring, of course, but try to add something green, red, yellow, purple, and orange to the mix. The technical term for the beneficial ingredients in colorful foods is *phytonutrients*, which produce the distinctive bright colors in fruits and vegetables. Phytonutrients have antioxidant properties that will protect your body from toxic free radicals, which are thought to play a role in aging, as well as in other degenerative diseases.

Exercise

As I mentioned, running is my physical drug of choice, but whatever you do, getting your heart pumping and your body moving is one of the best ways to reduce stress and elevate your mood. It doesn't matter what you do, as long as you are moving. Don't start any physical program without consulting your doctor first, but here are some suggestions once you get the go-ahead from your physician.

- **Join a walking group**. Whether it's around the park or around the mall, whenever your feel tense or anxious—walk it off! The higher you get your pulse going, the better it is for your heart.
- **Dance**. For some people, exercise is an anathema. For these couch potatoes, I suggest doing something fun, such as dancing. Try hip-hop, ballroom, or Zumba, or put on your favorite music and get moving.   Dancing is a great release, physically, emotionally, and creatively.
- **Join a team sport.** Women are still not as likely to get involved in team sports as men (although this is rapidly changing), and, as a result, we lose out on that feeling of camaraderie and morale boosting that comes with helping or cheering on a fellow player. Because alcoholics feel isolated from the world, nothing could be better than joining a soccer group, a tennis or golf club, or a softball or volleyball team. You will meet other women who are physically fit, competitive (for the type A's among us), and playful. To celebrate a win or comfort a loss, go for smoothies afterward, instead of hanging out at a sports bar.

Laugh

Scientific evidence demonstrates the healing powers of laughter, so the more humor you have in your life, the better it is for your recovery and your general well-being. So much so, that there is now a group of comedians who call themselves the Recovery Comics. They are on a mission to spread the healing power of laughter to everyone in recovery or in need. They do their stand-up acts at rehab facilities or national recovery conventions around the country and are available for private events, should your program or AA group want to book them for a fund-raising event. If you would like to schedule the Recovery Comics for a fund-raiser or just for fun, e-mail comedytogoinc@yahoo.com, or call 516-232-3222.

You can also go with friends to a regular comedy club in your town or city, but order seltzer or cranberry juice as part of the two-drink minimum. Don't forget to tip the waiters generously to compensate for the inexpensive nonalcoholic beverages!

11

Staying Sober: Alcoholics Anonymous and Other Programs

It helps to learn the difference between being responsible to others and being responsible for others.
—Alcoholics Anonymous

Alcoholics Anonymous (AA) is one of the largest and most respected support groups for drinkers in the world. Millions of people, including many of the women interviewed in this book, have found it to be the anchor that helps them stay grounded in sobriety. AA meetings are free, and, if you are medically stable, they can be an alternative to costly residential treatment centers. Founded in 1935 by Bill Wilson and Dr. Bob Smith, AA was first created to serve a white male Protestant population. AA eventually opened its doors to women and people of all stripes and beliefs (the first female member, Florence Rankin, joined in 1936). Today, the single requirement for membership is a desire to stop drinking. AA's name was derived from the book originally titled *Alcoholics Anonymous: The Story of How More Than*

One Hundred Men Have Recovered from Alcoholism, which was later revised and updated to include its diverse and expanding membership. It is now commonly known as the Big Book. (To read portions of the Big Book, go to www.anonpress.org.)

AA is run by its members, instead of by professionals, and its twelve-step program has been adopted by other support groups, such as Narcotics Anonymous, Overeaters Anonymous, and Gamblers Anonymous. The twelve steps are a way for members to build character and receive spiritual guidance by, among other things, admitting to their addiction without the fear of outing themselves publicly, making reparations to people they have hurt, finding and/or becoming a sponsor, and attending meetings to sustain a kinship with, and the support of, their fellow alcoholics. Those who stay in the program also receive chips marking the length of their sobriety. According to a recent three-year study, continuous involvement in AA or other twelve-step programs was the greatest predictor of sustained sobriety for female alcoholics.

Another reason for AA's longevity and success is that it teaches members crucial coping skills that they can use to stay sober. The tenth step, for example, asks members to take a personal inventory of when they do something wrong and promptly admit to it. Taking a daily inventory of your actions and behaviors makes it possible to avoid wallowing in guilt and shame during a lapse in judgment. As it says in the *Twelve Steps and Twelve Traditions of Alcoholics Anonymous*, "Learning daily to spot, admit, and correct these flaws is the essence of character-building and good living. . . . An honest regret for harms done, a genuine gratitude for blessings received, and a willingness to try for better things tomorrow will be the permanent assets we shall seek."

Another important coping skill, which seems to resonate with women in AA, is the concept of humility. In this case, it is not the self-effacing kind that women who defer their needs to others know all too well. It's the willingness to honestly examine their resentments, self-pity, and pride, which prevent them from asking for help from others. Because women are socialized to help others, it is often difficult for them to accept help *from* others. AA shows women that they must be humble enough to admit that recovery is not something they can do on their own.

Alcoholics Anonymous also promises members certain rewards in life should they manage to stick with the program. These "promises," as stated in the Big Book, include: "Knowing a new freedom and happiness. We will not regret the past nor wish to shut the door on it. We will comprehend the word *serenity* and we will know peace. No matter how far down the scale we have gone, we will see how our experiences can benefit others. That feeling of uselessness and self-pity will disappear. We will lose interest in selfish things and gain interest in our fellows. Self-seeking will slip away. Our whole attitude and outlook upon life will change."

Although this might seem like a tall order for women alcoholics who are still struggling with their shame and guilt, many who have gone through the program have testified that if you stay the course, these promises will, in fact, be fulfilled. Despite its successes, AA is not for everyone, and there is a 64 percent dropout rate in the first year, which is why I have provided alternative support groups in "Getting Help" at the end of the book.

Why Some Women Are Wary of AA

One of the biggest fears women alcoholics have is being found out. Yet even if you do run into people you know, what happens at meetings stays at the meetings. Plus, if someone you know is there, then she or he is also an alcoholic, which means you have something, albeit terrible, in common. That person is probably just as frightened of having her secret revealed as you are. Chances are, whoever knows you probably already suspects that you have a drinking problem, so who are you fooling? Remember, there is nothing shameful about asking for help. In fact, getting and staying sober is something you should be proud of!

There are two basic kinds of AA meetings: discussion and speaker. A speaker meeting is one in which members are encouraged to stand up in front of the room and "share" personal stories about their alcoholism and how they managed to get and stay sober. The speakers are usually chosen ahead of time, so you would not be asked or expected to speak as a newbie or a first-timer. Should that happen, however, all you need to say is, "No, thank you." You are not even expected to introduce yourself if you don't want to.

Speaker meetings allow you to listen to others who have probably had similar experiences to your own. If you are nervous about going to your first meeting, take a seat in the back of the room and leave as soon as the meeting is over. You might pick up some tips from other alcoholics, which is one reason support groups work so well.

Discussion groups are more personal and interactive. They usually involve a chairperson, who will open the meeting by making announcements or by reading from the Big Book, frequently from the section on "How It Works." Members might sit around a table, in a circle of chairs, or facing a podium. Topics could include "triggers," "cravings," and "gratitude," or there may be a discussion about one of the twelve steps. In other words, it's a bit like belonging to a book club. The chairperson will moderate the discussion, ask for volunteers who want to share, or simply go in order around the room.

Here, you are expected to introduce yourself (first name only) before speaking. Once everyone who wants to speak has had a chance, the meeting is adjourned. Before everyone leaves, however, a basket or a can might be passed around for those who wish to donate. The money pays for the room rental, beverages, snacks, and any AA-generated literature, which you should take with you, along with a copy of the Big Book. As in most houses of worship, all contributions are entirely voluntary.

You might not like the first meeting you go to, but don't let that discourage you from trying again or going on another night, when the group dynamic might be different. It's similar to looking for a good doctor: you shouldn't hesitate to shop around and ask for recommendations. When you first quit drinking and you are not in a residential treatment center, it is recommended that you go to a meeting every day. Yes, you read that correctly: every single day. Some people go more than once a day. Women often need that reinforcement, especially in the beginning, but the more time you spend thinking about *not* drinking, the less time you will spend thinking about alcohol.

AA as a Religious Organization

There have always been questions about AA being a "religious" organization, but it is not about religion or theology—it's about spirituality. Many women suffer from so much shame about the decisions they have made and the negative behavior they engaged in as a result of their alcoholism that the idea of living by spiritual principles can be intimidating and overwhelming. Nevertheless, studies and anecdotal evidence clearly show that having a spiritual foundation, whether or not it is part of an organized religion, is a significant part of long-term recovery.

That said, God, as you understand Him, is a big part of AA, and members will talk a lot about praying, divine intervention, and being "saved," so if this makes you uncomfortable, AA might not be for you. In fact, most meetings end by everyone standing and holding hands and reciting a prayer, such as the following:

Serenity Prayer
God grant me the serenity
to accept the things I cannot change;
courage to change the things I can;
and wisdom to know the difference

Again, you are not required to participate in this ritual, but if you don't want to feel like the odd woman out, you can remain silent with your head appropriately bowed. Similar to sports fans cheering their team on, some AA members like to end meetings by chanting, "Keep coming back, it works!" Most people find these communal rituals inspirational, but, again, you must work within your own level of comfort.

Most of the women interviewed for this book, as well as those whom I have worked with as a therapist and an educator, say that living a more spiritual life has helped them stay sober. I am not talking about religion or even religious principles. It's a matter of being grounded in the belief that something out there is bigger and more powerful than you. Call it what you want: God, the universe, the cosmic tumblers, the sacred vortex. Find something that you can believe in and begin to put your faith in it. You haven't done such a great job of tackling your alcoholism on your own—why not let something bigger than yourself intercede?

AA refers to the alcoholic as someone for whom "self-will has run riot." The idea of living a more spiritual way of life can be a stumbling block for many of us entering recovery, but I assure you that it is neither painful nor impossible. Start by relying on something other than your own stubborn will. Take down your protective shield so that you can turn your problem into a great opportunity.

The usual price of admission toward achieving a whole new level of sobriety is your self-will, and the spiritual elements of AA are based on a belief in some kind of higher power. If you don't believe in God, commit yourself instead to the principles of honesty, humility, and tolerance. The advice I give women who are struggling with this aspect of AA is simple: work hard on your recovery, don't lie, and be kind to those around you. Can you do that? If so, this can be the beginning of your journey toward living a more spiritual life. Women who readily embrace the spiritual aspects of AA often kick it up a notch by also attending Bible study or prayer groups, by learning how to meditate, and, as I will discuss later, by serving others.

Loving Sobriety

Here are one woman's thoughts about her newfound sobriety.

I'm thirty days sober today, and what a wonderful feeling that is! It's hard to believe the difference that not drinking has made to my life. The improvements are incredible. I feel so peaceful almost all of the time. I was constantly anxious and fearful, and now I feel calm and wonderfully content. I don't waste time worrying and fretting about things over which I have no control. I can deal with life so much better already and have found the Serenity Prayer really helpful when problems come along. I smile and laugh so much more.

Today I feel serenity gently glowing inside me. I have a new addiction: sobriety. I have never felt so good in my entire life. I can hardly believe that I'm actually saying any prayers at all—this is totally alien to me, but I'm desperate enough not to drink again, to just try my best to do as I'm advised. If praying is going to keep me sober, then that is what I will do. I know for a fact that I can't stay sober on my own. If standing on my head would keep me sober, I would do it.

FAQs about AA

Will I be able to smoke?

As much as I would like you to give up cigarettes, along with the booze, I realize that not everyone can handle getting rid of two addictions at once. Yet the days of smoke-filled meeting rooms and overflowing ashtrays are over. You might be able to find a meeting where smoking is still allowed, but your best bet is to take your cigarette break outside or in a designated area.

Can I go to a meeting if I think I'm a borderline alcoholic?

First of all, being a borderline alcoholic is like being "a little bit pregnant." If you suspect that you have a drinking problem, you probably do. That said, declaring yourself an "alcoholic" is not a requirement for AA membership. You must simply have a desire to quit drinking. Many people go to meetings and continue to drink—it's about the process, the steps, the support, breaking through the wall of your denial, quitting, and continued sobriety.

Be aware, however, that attendees will introduce themselves by saying, "Hello, I'm Kitty, and I'm an alcoholic." If you are not ready to admit your problem or are simply unsure about your status, you might want to say instead: "Hello, my name is Kitty, and I don't know if I'm an alcoholic," or, "I'm Kitty, and this is my first time here."

Are the meetings necessary? I need to spend that time with my family.

Were you spending time with your family while you were drinking? Were you actually present while you were obsessing about alcohol—wondering when, how, or where you were going to get that next drink? You must be willing to do whatever it takes to stay sober, even if that means spending an hour (that's how long the typical meeting lasts) at an AA meeting.

Finding a Sponsor

Getting a sponsor is one of the core principles of the AA recovery program. You must be willing and able to confide in someone about your fears, shame, anger, and disappointment. As I've said repeatedly, alcoholism is an isolating disease, so your recovery depends on reconnecting with the sober world. Reconnecting is essential to building your resilience.

A sponsor should be someone who has been sober for at least one year, and some AA groups suggest between four and ten years. Most recovering alcoholics will boast about how long they've been sober, so this is a good way to find out whether someone has sponsor potential. If you are not sure, ask directly after the meeting is over. You can go up to the person and say, "I'm new here, and I was moved by what you said at the meeting. Would it be all right if I ask how long you've been sober?"

Your sponsor can guide you through the twelve steps, introduce you to other AA members, and give you advice about what has helped her stick to the program. In other words, she is your mentor in recovery. She is someone whom you can count on, day or night, to talk you out of taking that drink and is always a phone call, an e-mail, or a text message away. You must be honest with your sponsor, as if she were a counselor. If you've fallen off the wagon, she will help you climb back on. She has the power to call you on your bad behavior and is willing to risk your drunken wrath in order to help you find a new way of living.

Some women reject the idea of having a sponsor because they get their hackles up whenever people tell them what to do. To this, I say, "Get over yourself. You're an alcoholic, and you haven't done too well on your own, so it's time to let someone who has been to hell and back be your role model for recovery." If you are *not* choosing an AA member as a mentor, stay clear of so-called enablers, who unwittingly support your drinking. You need to choose someone who is strong enough to stand up to you, should you be defensive or resistant, and to help you with some tough love. Don't be afraid to call on your sponsor when you are in need. You are not being a burden because sponsorship is a two-way street, and you are actually helping your mentor as much as she is helping you.

As with choosing the right doctor, finding a sponsor might be difficult at first, so if you have trouble, keep looking and don't give up until you find a good fit. Hopefully, you will be a sponsor to someone else one day and will know firsthand what it feels like to guide newbies out of the dark cave of alcoholism.

One of the true giants in the field of alcoholism and recovery was Father Joseph Martin. Early in my recovery, I attended a conference where he was the speaker, and I had the good fortune of being able to spend some time with him. I asked him what he thought was the most important aspect of staying sober. He looked at me, a fledgling in this journey, being only six months sober, and said, "Having a really good sponsor who will teach you the way." I have always held those words of wisdom dear, and I pass them on to you as you begin this journey.

It is a good idea to select a woman as a sponsor to avoid any potential sexual tension that might interfere with the dynamics of your mentor/mentee relationship. Many people have been known to find their future partners at AA meetings. This is fine, but keep in mind that AA is not a dating service (although there are online dating services for recovering alcoholics). Your sponsor should be someone who will lead by example and will call you on your behavior should you step out of line. As Father Martin said, "You are the student, Grasshopper, and your sponsor is your teacher."

Another good way to find a mentor is to announce that you are looking for a sponsor on an interim or permanent basis and see who steps up to the plate. Of course, that leaves it up to others coming forward, rather than your making a selection. Chances are, more than one person will volunteer, so you can choose from that pool of candidates. If you want to be more proactive and select someone yourself, you can start by observing people during meetings and chatting with fellow members until you find someone you think would be right for the job. You could ask a person you are interested in recruiting whether she has ever sponsored someone before or simply say, "Would you be interested in sponsoring me?" Please don't take it personally if you get a few rejections. Maybe that woman isn't ready to take on the responsibility, or perhaps she is already sponsoring more than one person and doesn't have time to give you the attention you need. You don't want anyone who is on the fence.

Finally, make sure that your sponsor is committed to the program. She must attend meetings regularly, as well as other AA functions, such as conferences, retreats, and volunteer work. Although it's okay to pick a relative or a friend as part of your support group, an AA sponsor in the traditional sense should be someone who knows the drill and can help you become more familiar with the program. Plus, you might not feel comfortable confiding your deepest, darkest secrets to a close friend or a family member, and part of having a sponsor is the ability to be completely open and honest with her about your past, present, and future. Don't muck up the relationship by bringing in your aunt Lilly, who might tell your sister or mother some personal details when asked for a progress report. Despite these caveats, the amazing thing about AA sponsorship is that it works and has been working for more than a half century!

DON'T ARGUE WITH THE INNER VOICE

The following story by Shelly Marshall, an addiction specialist at Day By Day, Recovery Resources, illustrates the importance of listening to that small voice inside you, instead of fighting it.

The principle of listening for inner guidance and acting on that guidance has been the cornerstone of my spiritual growth. I have often heard, "Listen to that still, small voice," and yet I haven't always had the courage to do what must be done. Long ago, when I first tried to get off drugs and alcohol, I made a deal with that still small voice: I would be of service to others and the voice inside would keep me on the path of sobriety. The voice, whether it's my Higher Power, higher self, or some type of angel, has never failed to prompt, protect, and propel me along a clean and sober path these last 39 years. Not to say I haven't argued with that pesky voice from time to time. The first "message" from my new-found friend, came early in sobriety. . . . At a 12th Step Club, my inner voice urged me to ask Elaine, my friend's mom, to sponsor me. I didn't really know this strait-laced, prudish woman, but she had gotten sober through AA and had recently lost her young son to drugs. We had nothing in common. I didn't want to ask. But the words blurted out, unbidden by me,

"Will you be my sponsor?" She politely declined, and I left the club thoroughly embarrassed and feeling betrayed by my inner guidance. That evening she phoned.

"This has never happened to me before," Elaine explained, "but my Higher Power brought me to my knees and told me, "I am not sending you sponsees for them, I am sending them for you." Her voice trembled. "I would be honored to be your sponsor, if you will still have me." That was her first lesson for me— don't argue with the inner voice! This loving, spiritual, newly grieving woman devoted her time to helping me stay sober. Others came. One young woman after another sought sobriety through her inspiring words until she was sponsoring 10 of us. She no longer had room for grief, but took joy in our progress and emerging spirituality. We learned so many things from her— honesty, open-mindedness, how to be of service to others and how to follow the promptings of our inner voice. To us, she was an angel sent from God.

Through the loving guidance of Elaine, practicing the principles of the program and doing the next right thing, I have
attempted to listen and serve on the whispers of the still small
voice within. People sometimes call me crazy or weird because
they can't see the larger picture—but then often I don't see that
picture either. I end up doing some things that puzzle me and
I'm sure others, but I do it on faith and trust nonetheless.

Twenty-one years after Elaine's son died, I received a call
from one of the people she sponsored. "Elaine is in the hospital,"
she said. "She has been diagnosed with lung cancer. She'll be
home in a few days and they say she has four months. We
thought you should know."

I started crying because I knew she was going soon and
because I was so far away and couldn't be there to help. Then a
small voice whispered inside. I recognized it immediately as her
son, Johnny's voice—he spoke firmly and plainly, "Please buy
some Lilies of the Valley, and send them to Mother. Write on the
card, 'I'm waiting for you' and sign my name."

Talk about arguing with an inner voice! Boy did I argue. It
made it sound like she was going to die right away—it sounded
weird again. But Johnny insisted and was urgent. "Please," he
begged. In the end I did it, but I didn't put what he asked me to,
I simply signed his name.

There was an immediate outcry from the other sponsees.
"How could she?" they railed. "How cruel!" and they refused to
let me speak to her to explain. They "protected" Elaine from me
and not one had the courage to talk to me about it.

Elaine died within 24 hours after receiving the flowers. She
never made it home. I like to think she had an epiphany and
quickly understood her son really did send the flowers and was
waiting for her. I like to think she let go sooner than expected
because she wanted to go to him. I like to think Johnny and
Elaine are grateful for my service and courage. I paid a price,
though. Mainly, that some women who were once dear to me
chose never to speak to me again. They even refused to give me
a few small mementos she had left for each of us. I think about
that day once in a while and about what I would do differently
today.

I would have signed just what Johnny told me; I would not
edit the message. I'm sure Elaine felt weird too about taking so

much joy in her sponsees so soon after the death of her son. Many years ago, she gave me the courage to go forth into life and live it clean and sober. I can only hope I gave her the same courage to go forth into the next life into the loving arms of her son. Her final lesson to me: Don't argue with the inner voice.

Working with a Sponsor

Once you find your sponsor, don't wait until you get an urge to drink before calling her. It's important to build up a connection with this person as you spend more time at meetings and go through the twelve steps. Some sponsors will tell you to check in with them at least once a day so that you can both see how things are going. If you get into the habit of talking when all is well, you will be more likely to call if you start having second thoughts. If your sponsor doesn't recommend these probation phone meetings, politely ask whether it would be all right if you called once or twice a week, at least in the beginning. Most sponsors will readily agree to that. You don't have to chat for long, and it doesn't have to be about drinking—you can tell her what you are up to that day. The point is that you are establishing a relationship and trust.

You might also suggest going to coffee before or after meetings, so that you can have some face time when you can ask questions and get better acquainted. You can use this time to discuss things that have been upsetting you, any triggers that you might be struggling with, as well as your cravings. Many sponsors will wait for you to reach out to them, and you won't hear from them unless you initiate the call. You can discuss this in advance and figure out what arrangement works best for you.

Should you come to loggerheads with your sponsor because she is telling you what she thinks you should do based on her own experience, remember that she has managed to get and stay sober, and you are still in the nascent stages, so it might not be a bad idea to listen closely to what she has to say. It's also okay to change sponsors if you find that you are not a good match with a certain person. You can search for a new sponsor first, then inform the other one that you have found someone new, or you can have more than one sponsor. Likewise, it's okay for a sponsor to have several sponsees. I know it sounds a bit polygamous, but as long as you are open and honest with your sponsors, and everyone is fine with it, it's okay.

For more information about sponsors, get and read the pamphlet called "Questions and Answers about Sponsorship" at your local AA office or meeting.

Being a Sponsor

This post from pocketsponsor.com reiterates how rewarding sponsorship can be.

Being a sponsor in any 12 Step program is absolutely the highest honor I can think of in recovery. Sponsoring other people makes each of us grow in ways we could have never dreamed of. They say that sponsorship is wonderful because you get to tell others what to do and if it works, you might try it! Okay, we know that isn't exactly the way it works, or at least we hope not! Yet my relationship with my sponsor was one of the most precious gifts I received coming into the fellowship.

Tips for Staying Sober

Remember the triggers I talked about in chapter 10? When these come on, and they will, you will be tempted to drink again. Yet here are several things you can do to distract yourself or diminish your cravings:

- **Drink water.** As much as you might want to reach for a soda, tea, or coffee, have one or two large glasses of water instead. Caffeine is a stimulating chemical that will disrupt your sleep. Being thirsty can set off a craving, so if you hydrate quickly with water, the desire for alcohol will often disappear or at least dissipate.
- **Call someone in your lifeline.** The next thing you must do is tell your sponsor or mentor that you are feeling the urge to drink again. Sometimes simply saying the words out loud

will help you get rid of the craving. If you don't reach your sponsor right away, call back or keep going down your lifeline list until you reach a living, breathing sober person.

- **Go to a meeting**. You should also get yourself to a meeting—fast—should your craving occur during a time when a meeting is scheduled. Remember when you used to say, "It's 5 p.m. somewhere in the world," as you filled up your glass? Well, there's a meeting going on somewhere in the world, hopefully in your hometown, so the trick is to go out and find it when you are in need. This is why you should keep your AA meeting list close at hand. My sponsor used to tell me that there were only two times you should go to a meeting: every time that you want to and every time that you do not want to!

The First Thirty Days

A woman talks about how important a support network is.

The first week was easy . . . in the hospital. The rest was hard, but by being honest with myself, my friends, and my family I was able to get the support I needed. Also, going to at least one AA meeting per day gave me a great boost. There's nothing like having a group of people who are so willing to help and who truly understand what you're going through.

- **Change your location.** Sometimes being in a certain place at a certain time reminds you of your drinking days. If this happens, the best thing to do is immediately leave where you are and change the setting. Even going into a different room of the house can do the trick—let's say, getting out of the kitchen and going to the living room because you once stored your vodka in the pantry. Visit a friend. Get a manicure or a massage. Go to a restaurant and have a healthful snack. If you're sitting in front of the TV, clean the house instead. If you are at the computer working, go outside and weed the garden (city dwellers can go window shopping), go to a movie, or browse the self-help section of a bookstore. Remember that your cravings will soon pass. Keep a journal of your feelings, and make a note of what you did to battle your inner drinking demons.

- **Get moving**. One of the best and healthiest substitutes for drinking is exercise. When I stopped drinking, running was my way to relieve stress and anxiety. I believe that running was a large part of my early recovery. So, go to the gym, go for a run, or take a walk in the park, in the woods, or around the block. Getting your blood circulating through exercise, and the movement will release endorphins—your natural feel-good hormones—into your body. You might get tired if you exercise too strenuously, but you can't OD on endorphins!

- **Stay away from places where there is alcohol**. This might seem obvious, but when you first quit drinking, it is sometimes difficult to steer clear of places that carry or serve liquor. Imagine that alcohol has taken out a restraining order against you. This means avoiding the beer or wine section of your grocery store, declining invitations to social functions where you know there will be an open bar, and driving down another road to avoid passing your formerly favorite bar. It's worth the inconvenience. The good news is that once you are sober for a while, you will develop the willpower to be around others who drink without developing a craving. The phrase "No thank you" will trip easily off your tongue when someone offers you a drink.

- **Enjoy good clean fun**. I know that your idea of a good time used to mean getting smashed, but now you must find other ways to enjoy yourself. Go to a movie, a concert, an art gallery, or a show. Listen to music that inspires you. Take up painting, learn to play an instrument, or take a cooking class. Keep a journal or start a daily blog about your sobriety. You don't have to tell anyone about your blog; it can be for your eyes alone, or you can open it up to your support group and others who are struggling with addiction. People who search for words such as *sober* or *alcoholism* will find it. Engaging in an activity that lifts your spirit is a great way to break bad old habits and start having some good clean fun!

Having Fun Sober

Last week I saw a concert I'd been waiting for years to see. Had two soft drinks instead of something harder. It's nice not messing up a good evening. A good night was even better

- **Practice visualization**. It helps some women if they visualize a bottle of alcohol as something they find abhorrent. Whatever that repugnant object is for you, be it a spider, a snake, a rat, or a burning flame that will scorch you if touched, try this imaginary game whenever you see an alcoholic beverage. If someone asks you to hold her drink while she gets something to eat at a party, politely refuse by saying, "I'm sorry, but I must go to the ladies' room myself," or "I just got over a bad cold, and I don't want you to get my germs." You could also make sure that your hands are always full of appetizers, so that you won't be asked to carry anyone's drink.
- **Meditate**. Meditation and other relaxation techniques can help you control your thoughts, urges, and stress level. Meditation involves breathing and emptying your mind of all of the random thoughts (good and bad) that barrage you every second. It can be done lying down, sitting cross-legged on a mat or in a chair, or resting against a pillow, but you must find a quiet place where you are not interrupted by children, telephones, tweets, texts, television, and other outside stimuli.

  Once you have found your quiet retreat, take long deep breaths in through your nose and breathe out from your mouth. I recommend buying or renting a CD or a DVD or going online for more information on meditation or the relaxation response. There are even guided meditation classes, if you want to meditate in a group setting, or you could take yoga classes, which always end with a few minutes of deep relaxation.

It might be difficult to do at first, but don't give up! Being still is one of the hardest things to do in this multitasking world, especially for women, but meditation has been proved to be one of the best coping mechanisms around and has been practiced for thousands of years. (See "Getting Help" in the back of the book for recommended books and CDs.)

- **Remember the bad times**. Whenever you are tempted to slide, think about the negative consequences of your drinking—the vomiting, the hangovers, the headaches, the fighting, the hiding—and maybe your temptation will go away. Now, substitute those negative experiences with memories of when you were sober and having a good time with family or friends.

REMEMBERING THE BAD TIMES TO STAY SOBER

The hard times for me came sixty days after quitting, when I forgot about the bad hangovers and just remembered the taste. I've since made a mental image of the big-time sick headaches to remind me why I had to get sober.

Helping Others

As alcoholics we become egocentric, which means that everything is about me, me, me. Those in recovery must break out of this narcissistic pattern and start to think about ways they can be of service to others. Our isolation has put us back in that childish state of thinking about our immediate needs first and neglecting the people (and the world) around us.

Believe it or not, someone out there is in more pain than you are and could use your help. Use the time you wasted on being wasted and find a charity where you can volunteer. Aside from the great feeling you'll get from helping those in need, you are likely to meet new people whose values you can admire and emulate. Being of service to others is also a way of giving back to those who helped you through your troubled times. As you move though the recovery process, you sometimes forget how bad it was and what your life was like when you were at your lowest. Volunteering is an excellent way to work on your personal growth and to look at life's difficulties as opportunities to be of service to others. I spent several years volunteering at a soup kitchen, and it was an excellent reminder of how fortunate I was in so many ways. It taught me to always be mindful that I was given a second chance in life, thanks to my recovery.

Check your local listings for places to volunteer in your community, or go to www.volunteer.org to locate a charity near you.

Gratitude

The act of living in gratitude is a shield that protects us from our day-to-day struggles and pain. If I look at what my life would have been had I not stopped drinking and what it has become today, I am overcome by awe and gratitude. Gratitude has helped recovering women from relapsing into their old destructive behavior. Why? Because if you are grateful for all that you have and all that you have been given through recovery, it is difficult to encounter an obstacle that you cannot deal with.

At the end of the day, make a list of one or more things that you are grateful for or something that happened to you that day for which you would like to give thanks. You can also make your list in the morning, which is what I do. It helps me start my day off on the right track. You can include people on your list as well. To that end, you can take it a step further and write a quick "thank you" note or e-mail to the people to whom you are grateful. Keep your list simple. In the morning, you can be grateful for having had a restful night's sleep; at night, you can be grateful for the fact that you didn't drink today or for the friendly exchange you had with a neighbor. Once you start opening yourself up to observing the little gifts that come your way in your everyday life, you will find that your list will expand and you will notice even more of life's everyday miracles.

Gratitude is about looking at the positive, rather than at the negative. It means focusing on the gifts that you have received but did not necessarily deserve. I'm not suggesting that you will always have a good day, but noticing the good things that happen will help offset these negative experiences. Be willing to reconnect, to live by spiritual principles, to reach out and help others, and to be grateful for each and every day that you are not living with pain and humiliation. Remember, being sober is a reflection of your own will and efforts, as well as the grace of whatever power you summoned to help you in your journey toward a better self and a better life.

12

Family Matters

Although more men are stepping up as fathers and sharing the household duties, women are still the primary caregivers and, as a result, the cornerstones of their families' stability. When a woman is an alcoholic, however, her priorities change: she goes from putting her family first to putting her drinking first. Her energy is spent either hiding her addiction or rationalizing it. Most alcoholics aren't even aware that this is where much of their shame comes from. To that end, I have selected the most common rationalizations I have heard from women and teenage alcoholics during my career as an addiction counselor, and I explain how these excuses affect the delicate emotional balance within a family.

Rationalization: I only drink after the kids are in bed and my husband is on the computer or watching TV.

Reality check: Closet drinkers, as you remember from the first part of this book, will do whatever it takes to ensure that their kids, spouses, or friends do not discover their martini secret. Yet just because you are able to hide your drinking from your family doesn't mean they don't suspect that something's wrong with Mommy.

When your nurturing instincts, which most women possess, get drowned out by alcohol, you will inevitably begin to neglect your family. The third or fourth time you "forget" to pick the kids up after soccer practice or the fact that you no longer tuck your five-year-old into bed at night because you're busy getting wasted in the kitchen are red flags waving you in for help. Depending on how serious a woman alcoholic's drinking problem is, she is frequently unable to pack the kids' lunchboxes, clean the house, or ferry the children to and from playdates and other activities.

Although this kind of neglect might not be considered abusive behavior, it can eat away at children's feelings of self-worth because they are being ignored by the person who is supposed to love them the most. The message you are giving them is that they are not as important as alcohol. Maybe you haven't fallen down the stairs, but you've fallen down on your job as mother.

Rationalization: My husband likes it when I drink.

Reality check: While some husbands actually prefer their wives to be drunk because they believe the women are more fun to be with when tipsy, most men prefer wives who are mentally and physically in the game when it comes to the marriage. I knew one man who poured his wife a drink the day she got home from rehab because he liked her personality better when she was drunk. This kind of enabling is like being an accomplice to a crime. He might be driving the getaway car, instead of robbing the bank, but he's just as guilty. The phenomenon of the happy (but drunk) housewife might be one reason I have found that more divorces happen after recovery than during active addition. Yet the truth is that women alcoholics no longer want or need relationships with their husbands because their first and only love is with the bottle.

Rationalization: I'm able to drink and take care of my family. My kids have clean clothes and are getting their homework done.

Reality check: This is the credo held most often by the functional alcoholic. She is, in fact, able to maintain some version of normalcy by making sure that her family's needs are addressed. Unfortunately, it is all smoke and mirrors. The smoke will eventually fill the room and the mirrors will crack. Even if you are able to keep up this ruse for years, the slow progression of alcoholism will one day take over, simply because the longer you drink, the more you will need to sustain your addiction. Again, you are only fooling yourself if you believe that just because your kids look okay to the outside world, your entire inner world isn't coming apart at the seams.

Rationalization: Your husband tells your kids, "Your mom doesn't drink *that* much."

Reality check: In treatment parlance, this is called enabling, which is often done by members of the family who circle their wagons to protect the alcoholic. An enabler is someone who continues to accept bad behavior by making excuses for it. Sometimes enablers tell outright lies such as, "Your mom doesn't have a drinking problem, it's hormonal." Sometimes a husband will even call the woman's workplace to tell her boss that his wife is sick when in fact she can't get out of bed because of a hangover.

Although this behavior is well-intentioned, an alcoholic will never get better if people don't call her on her behavior. I'm not talking about making threats, such as, "I will leave you if you don't stop drinking," because if she continues to drink and the spouse doesn't leave, she will see his threats for what they are—empty. If you are living with an alcoholic woman, you must stop allowing her to get away with her drinking. You must gather together your family and friends and say, "We love you and care about you. What can we do to help?" Children can and should talk to a counselor, either at school or privately, about what's going on.

Another form of enabling is what I call the "don't ask, don't tell" approach. In this case, the husband will escape, instead of making excuses for or confronting the alcoholic. This approach never works because keeping everything locked away in the closet is another way of encouraging the behavior.

Rationalization: You are the one who made me drink!

Reality check: One of the most frustrating aspects of dealing with an alcoholic or an addict within a family is when she blames someone else for her problem. Alcoholics can lose their jobs and their homes, get kicked out of school, or even have their children removed and still insist that they did nothing wrong. If this happens to you, you need to take inventory of what you have done in the past and, as part of the twelve-step program suggests, make amends. You must accept responsibility for your actions, including your decision to self-medicate with alcohol.

Start by getting on the computer or taking out a pen and paper and making a list of everyone whom you have hurt as a result of your drinking. This is also known as the fourth step in the AA program. If this makes you feel angry, resentful, or victimized and you start to play the blame game again, remember that "why" you did it isn't as important as "what you did," at least for now. The next steps are about finding ways that you can make things better. As we tell our kids who have misbehaved, a meaningful apology isn't a bad place to start.

Rationalization: All of the other kids are drinking; my daughter is just doing what everyone else does.

Reality check: This, of course, is how a teen or a coed explains away her drinking problem to her concerned parents. Maybe the parents also engaged in *Animal House*–type behavior when they were in school and feel hypocritical about stopping what is considered by many to be an adolescent rite of passage.

Although I know all too well that our colleges and universities are filled with students who play drinking games such as Pass Out and Rehab, this doesn't make it okay. Your party girl is not only doing something that is against the law, if she is underage; she is also destroying a young brain that is still growing and developing. If you once drank or used drugs as a teenager, use your experiences as teachable material. Rather than hide your past from your daughter because you're afraid she'll accuse you of being a "do as I say, not as I did" parent, own up to it and tell her that if you had it to do again, you would have concentrated more on school than on partying.

Rationalization: You drink, too!

Reality check: Let's face it, we are an alcohol-loving nation, but healthy people know when they've had enough. Nonalcoholics don't drink and drive. They don't dream about their next drink.

They don't stock up on liquor so that they won't be seen making too many trips to the package store. They have a glass of wine with dinner, not a bottle of wine without a meal. They see cocktails as something to be enjoyed when celebrating or socializing with friends, not guzzled or knocked back until they and their drinking buddies pass out. Yes, the alcoholic might have family and friends who drink, but that doesn't make them drunks. If you happen to surround yourself with alcoholics, however, then make a pact that you will help one another recover together.

Rationalization: I don't have time to go into treatment.

Reality check: You'll have plenty of time on your hands if you don't stop drinking, because you could lose your job, your husband, and your kids as a result. As we know, the alcoholic can't keep drinking without negative consequences occurring. If it rains too much and your house is built on a slippery slope, there will be a mudslide.

Rationalization: I can't leave my children to go into rehab.

Reality check: You've already left them by drinking. One of the arrangements that family and friends need to make before an alcoholic goes to a treatment center is making sure the children will be taken care of while the mother is away.

Sins of the Mother

When children grow up in a household with a substance-abusing parent, they can develop problems that last a lifetime. Studies have shown that children of alcoholics are more likely to develop alcoholism as adults than are those who are not. They are at risk for depression and anxiety, and they often lack the proper social skills and coping skills. It's one thing to destroy your own life, but ask yourself whether you are willing to pass on your legacy of addiction to your children. If not, use this as motivation to stop drinking immediately, if not for your sake, then for the sake of your children and grandchildren.

Look into their sweet, innocent eyes. Understand that they are carrying the burden of your alcoholism on their tiny shoulders. If you are ashamed of how you behave when drunk, think about how your children feel when they come home from school to find their mother passed out on the couch. Think about how they feel when they can't ask their friends over for playdates or sleepovers because they are afraid of what you might do.

Author and therapist Sharon Wegsheider Cruz discovered that children of alcoholics and addicts take on four basic roles within the family. The first is that of the Family Hero, who is usually the eldest child. The Family Hero is a forty-year-old soul hidden in a ten-year-old body. This child takes on the parental role, becoming, out of necessity, as well as of sheer willpower, responsible and self-sufficient. The Family Heroes are the ones who clean the house, fix dinner, or take care of the younger children. The Heroes are usually overachievers who try to do everything right so that their mothers will love them. They are the good students and the sports stars. The alcoholic mother might look at this child as proof that she hasn't messed up as a parent after all.

The second role that children of addicts often play is that of the Scapegoat. These children are the ones who act out at school by failing, bullying, or skipping classes. They are like the misbehaving mothers' sidekicks and sometimes use and abuse alcohol or drugs themselves. These children try to refocus the attention on themselves so that no one has to face the real problem: the alcoholic mothers.

The third role is that of the Lost Child. Lost children are usually quiet and afraid to speak up because they are terrified about what trap door will open up next in their lives. These children escape by becoming invisible. They daydream, fantasize about happy events, read lots of books, or escape through TV. They deal with reality by withdrawing from it. They deny that they have any feelings and don't bother getting upset. These children grow up to be adults who find it difficult to express their emotions, and they often suffer from low self-esteem. They are terrified of intimacy and have relationship phobia, because who knows what their partners might do to them? They are withdrawn, shy, and socially isolated because that is the only way they know to protect themselves from getting hurt.

The final childhood role within the dysfunctional family is called the Mascot. This is the family cut-up and social director who uses humor as emotional ballast for his or her pain. As with the Scapegoat, Mascots think that if they make everybody laugh, maybe no one will notice that Mom is chugging a bottle of vodka. Like the rodeo clown who tries to divert the attention of the bull, these children believe they can create enough of a diversion to keep the mother from striking out in anger. This child takes responsibility for the emotional well-being of the family.

The Mascot becomes an adult who is valued for her kind heart, generosity, and ability to listen to others. Mascots spend their lives trying to please others, at the expense of their own needs. As adults, they find it easier to give love than to receive it. Sometimes history repeats itself when the adult Mascot gets involved in an abusive relationship in an attempt to "save" the other person.

Whatever role the children play within the alcoholic family, these kids need someone whom they can trust to talk to about what's going on at home. Relatives, friends, teachers, counselors, coaches, or school nurses can step in to help children in need and let them know that it's not their fault and they are not responsible for curing their mothers.

EXPLAINING ALCOHOLISM TO YOUR CHILDREN

Growing up with an alcoholic or a drug addict usually means living by the rule, "It is not all right to talk about drinking or using in my family." It is difficult to work through the loneliness, fear, and frustration that children feel when living with an addicted parent, but if you are an alcoholic, you shouldn't hide your past from them once they reach an age where they can understand that alcoholism is a disease. Encourage them to express their feelings about your behavior and how it hurt them. Continue to emphasize that "Mommy was sick, but she's better now, and she never, ever stopped loving you."

Don't be afraid to repeat the message that drinking is something you no longer engage in. Make sure you answer your children's questions honestly and as often as they ask them. You can also initiate the conversation whenever the opportunity arises, such as when you see someone who is drunk on TV or in the movies. A good time to talk is while driving in the car, because children often feel more comfortable talking when they are not making eye contact with a parent.

Here are ten helpful tips for talking to your kids about alcoholism:

1. Start early, but give age-appropriate information.
2. Initiate the conversation with your child.
3. Create an open environment.
4. Communicate your new values.
5. Listen to your child.
6. Try to be honest.
7. Be patient.
8. Use everyday opportunities as "teachable moments."
9. Do not be defensive if your child expresses anger.
10. Talk about it again and again and again.

Games Husbands Play

Aside from the children, who suffer greatly from their mother's alcohol abuse, the spouse can play a crucial role in "enabling" or unwittingly encouraging his partner's drinking. Here are some of the ways that this is done.

The Rescuer

The Rescuer does everything in his power to protect the drinker so that her alcoholism doesn't become known outside the family. He will wait up for her to come home if she is out drinking with friends and will put her to bed if she is unable or in no condition to undress herself. If she passes out, he will pick her up, clean her up, and make her coffee. (Note: Drinking coffee or taking a cold shower will not sober you up because neither does anything to change the alcohol levels in the blood. You will still be drunk, only more awake and drunk.)

The Rescuer will go to great lengths to make sure the neighbors don't see his intoxicated wife passed out on the front porch. He never mentions the incident to anyone. If someone brings it up, he will deny or lie about the problem. Yet as the drinking gets worse, he will also be forced to take on the responsibilities that were once his wife's, such as getting the kids dressed for school, doing the laundry, or helping with the homework. If the alcoholic gets in trouble with the law, he will be right there digging into his pockets to bail her out.

The Provoker

The Provoker reacts by punishing the drunk for her actions. He might wait until the sober light of day to let her have it with both barrels blasting. He'll yell, ridicule, nag, and belittle, in the hope that his negative reaction will cause her to come to her senses. Unlike the Rescuer, he won't care if others hear him screaming. He might even tell his friends and other family members what a loser his wife is, in order to get sympathy. He is angry and wants the alcoholic and everybody else to know it. Some provokers even threaten to leave. If he stays, and many do, the anger and resentment continue to build as these incidents become more frequent. He will never let the alcoholic forget her transgressions. He keeps a laundry list of misbehaviors that he holds against her as a weapon in future arguments. This can go on for years, because the shame and guilt that the Provoker makes his wife feel will cause her to drink even more.

The Martyr

The Martyr is deeply ashamed of the alcoholic's behavior and will let her know it through his actions and words. Although not as hostile as the Provoker, he will tell her, "You've embarrassed us again in front of all of our friends!" He will sulk, pout, and isolate her physically and emotionally. Another more passive-aggressive type of Martyr will slowly become more withdrawn and will let her know by his actions that he is ashamed of her. He might not say anything directly to the alcoholic, but he will get on the phone or e-mail his friends to describe the misery that she has caused him. All of this makes her feel even more depressed and guilty, thus fueling the cycle.

Family Intervention

Technically, an intervention is anything that breaks the compulsive cycle and convinces the alcoholic to get some help. It ranges from one-on-one talks with a concerned friend to getting arrested for a DUI. It took my father coming to my house and asking, "Kitty, what's wrong?" to get me into treatment. Nowadays, however, interventions are thought of as a gathering of family members, friends, neighbors, and others who confront the alcoholic and try to get her into treatment. An intervention should *always* be done out of love and concern—not out of anger or revenge.

Ideally, an intervention, which is always a surprise, should be planned in advance with nearly the same attention to detail that one would devote to a wedding. I'm not talking about the menu and the dinnerware, of course, but having a treatment center lined up and ready to admit the alcoholic, the alcoholic's bags packed, and the transportation arranged to take her to the rehab or a treatment facility. I wouldn't have more than eight people at an intervention, and I do not believe children younger than eighteen should attend because it is too emotionally wrenching for them to see their mother in this vulnerable state. Even adolescents must be emotionally stable enough to handle an intervention.

Typically, people at an intervention will go around the room and talk about how much they love and care about the alcoholic and describe exactly what terrible things she has done as a result of her drinking. The husband might say, for instance: "Honey, the last time we went out for dinner, you had eight drinks and started making a scene in the restaurant." The rules of an intervention require people to cite specific behavior, rather than making general statements such as, "You've been acting like an idiot," or, "I heard you've been drinking too much." Participants must use personal experiences that they've had with the alcoholic that clearly show that her drinking has gotten out of control.

Enablers should never be present at an intervention. A typical enabler might say, "Well, you really aren't *that* bad." Family members and friends must be willing to be honest about what is happening and not flip-flop, or else the intervention won't work. The same goes for people who are also alcoholics. They need to have their own separate interventions or be willing to give up booze themselves.

It helps to have a professional leading the intervention, but it's not absolutely necessary. You can hire an intervention specialist or a counselor to walk you through the process and coach the family ahead of time. This person can engage you in a role-play by rehearsing your comebacks to certain responses. Whether or not the professional is present at the intervention, he or she can show you how to navigate this extremely stressful situation and will help you prepare for all possible outcomes. I suggest writing down what you are going to say and reading aloud from your notes or letter at the intervention so that you don't freeze up when you get there. It doesn't matter how you communicate your memories and feelings, as long as you are confident and strong.

Should the alcoholic refuse to go into treatment, for example, the family has to agree on what the consequences will be. If the alcoholic says, "This is a bunch of BS," the husband can say, "Okay, but I have hired an attorney to draw up divorce papers, and I intend to sign them and get full custody of the children." Really good interventions must have teeth, and you can't be afraid to use them. The alcoholic must realize the choice is between getting help or losing her family and friends. It's that simple. You cannot sit by and watch someone kill herself and bring the rest of the family down with her.

Let her know what her options are. If residential treatment is not on the table, going to a counselor or to an outpatient facility should be given as a choice. Whatever you think is appropriate or warranted is fine, as long as the desired outcome is established ahead of time, but don't allow her to put off getting treatment. If she says, "Okay, I'll see a therapist next week," you must counter by saying, "No, I've already made an appointment with a counselor for 4 p.m. today."

Try to keep the intervention limited to no more than an hour. If you can't reach the alcoholic in that amount of time, it's probably not going to happen. You don't want to beat her down to the point that she doesn't believe she can get well.

The bottom line is that interventions are, as the saying goes, about hating the sin but loving the sinner. Sure, there will be anger and hurt within that room, but it's not about shaming or blaming the alcoholic. If you no longer love the alcoholic, do not join the group. A successful staged intervention will not work if you are trying to shame the person into quitting. All of the participants should be saying, "I love you, I'm worried about you; what can I do to help?"

TIPS FOR A SUCCESSFUL INTERVENTION

To recap, following are some tips for planning an intervention, which might just help save your loved one's life:

1. Hire a professional interventionist. Evidence shows that interventions work best when directed by someone who specializes in addictions. Check the intervention specialist's background and ask for recommendations before you hire him or her.

2. Base the intervention on what has happened in the alcoholic's life, such as stealing, lying, neglect, or being arrested for driving under the influence. Research shows that an alcoholic is more willing to admit to her drinking problem and get help after a particular incident has occurred.

3. Make sure she is not drinking during the intervention. If possible, choose a time (mornings are best) and a place where you are certain she cannot obtain alcohol. If there are any signs of recent alcohol use, it's best to reschedule the intervention.

4. Be patient. The alcoholic will likely yell, scream, argue, and deny everything that's being said during the intervention (or she might completely shut down and withdraw). Stay calm and let the intervention specialist handle any conflicts that arise. The success of an intervention depends greatly on the willingness and the ability of family and friends to confront the addict. The alcoholic may resent you after the intervention, even if she agrees to get treatment. If this happens, try to remain positive and keep thinking of the ultimate goal: recovery.

5. Keep in mind that an intervention is only the first step in the alcoholic's recovery, because she must now go through detox and therapy and change her life in order to remain sober. It's helpful if you and other family members attend support group meetings and group therapy with your loved one.

She's Getting Treatment; Now What?

Interventions will help get an alcoholic into treatment, but what happens post-treatment when the recovering mother or daughter is back home? There are two support groups that I highly recommend, which help families and friends of alcoholics cope with the before, during, and after periods of recovery.

Al-Anon/Alateen

For more than fifty years, Al-Anon (which includes Alateen for younger members) has been offering support for friends and families of problem drinkers. Members include parents, children, spouses, partners, siblings, aunts and uncles, cousins, friends, and even coworkers of alcoholics. The organization estimates that every alcoholic affects the lives of at least four other people, making alcoholism a "family disease." No matter what your specific experience has been, everyone shares a common bond with those whose lives have been affected by someone else's drinking. Whether or not the alcoholic is still drinking, all who have been affected by her drinking can find solutions and, hopefully, serenity in the Al-Anon/Alateen fellowship.

One of Al-Anon's mottos is to "detach with love," and it teaches family members how to lift the responsibility for the alcoholic off their shoulders and to start thinking and caring about their own needs. When there is an alcoholic in the household, frequently everything revolves around that person. When is she drinking, what is she drinking, and how can we tiptoe around her so that she won't lash out at us when she's drunk? Al-Anon helps families take this focus off the alcoholic, while suggesting ways to get her into treatment or to support her in recovery.

Al-Anon also helps family and friends learn how to stop enabling the alcoholic by saying and doing things that might unwittingly encourage the alcoholic to drink. As a therapist and someone in recovery, I believe that the alcoholic is never 100 percent to blame for her condition. Spouses or parents should consider what, if anything, they have done that might have played a part in fueling the alcoholic's behavior. (For meeting information, you can call 888-4AL-ANON [888-425-2666] Monday through Friday, 8 a.m. to 6 p.m. EST. See the "Getting Help" section for more contact information.)

Families Anonymous

Similar to Al-Anon/Alateen, Families Anonymous (FA) is based on the twelve-step paradigm for concerned relatives and friends of someone with alcohol or addiction problems. In FA, members share their experiences with one another, in the hope that they will gather strength and support from each story. You will meet others who share your feelings and frustrations, if not your exact situation, which can help lessen some of the stigma and shame that families often feel while living with an alcoholic. The members understand that families are also shocked and annoyed by the person's refusal to get help and that they are sometimes resented for their efforts to get the sick person into treatment. You will learn how to have a better quality of life and to find some kind of resolution—whether your daughter is still drinking or is in recovery.

"We learn from our own experience," the FA website explains, "but we can also get a great deal of benefit from the shared misery and foolish mistakes we make while trying to do the best we possibly can do. That realization, in itself, goes a long way in helping us to start feeling good about ourselves . . . and, amazingly, sets the stage for the recovery."

Postrecovery Breakups

Many families think that when a woman gets sober, it will solve all of their problems, yet it can actually expose the underlying causes for the alcoholism. When the woman is an alcoholic, getting sober can drastically change the family dynamics, sometimes at the expense of the marriage. If she is drinking all of the time, she is often more dependent on her husband and might have isolated herself from the outside world because she found it impossible to do anything else.

Maybe she was willing to do whatever her husband told her to do, for fear of rocking an already unsteady boat. Now, she is no longer in such a precarious situation. Once a woman has undergone counseling, she is working through many of the issues that contributed to her desire or perceived need to drink in the first place, one of which might be an unhappy marriage. If she was being verbally abused, she might begin to stand up for herself, instead of self-medicating her pain with alcohol. Her husband is suddenly faced with a totally transformed person—someone he doesn't recognize or no longer likes. She may have been in a fog due to her drinking but now doesn't use alcohol as a way to cope anymore, so she is able to take a clear-eyed look at her relationship.

This is why there are more divorces during recovery than while the alcoholic is drinking. Wives in recovery are often unwilling to put up with their husbands' infidelity. When they're drunk, they think, "Do what you want, as long as I've got my wine." Or, the guilt and shame they felt while drinking forced them to accept their husbands' unacceptable behavior. In some cases, husbands actually liked it when their wives were sloshed because they were more fun to be with or didn't nag them as much.

The same goes for certain teenagers, who prefer it when their mother drinks because she stops supervising their behavior. This gives the teen freedom to break curfew or act out in other ways. The fact is, drunks care about one thing and one thing only—alcohol—so when the mother is drinking, she is less likely to notice if her children's rooms are a mess or if they've done their homework. When Mom is sober, she starts to pay attention once again to what's going on in her children's lives, and some adolescents resent the intrusion, which is otherwise known as good parenting.

Jealousy

Another problem that occurs within the family during the recovery stage, especially early on, is when husbands get jealous of their wives' newfound community of fellow alcoholics. After treatment, the wife is suddenly going to meetings once a week, once a day, or even several times a day, depending on the severity of her drinking problem, and she is no longer as available to her husband (as much as a raging alcoholic can be available). The secrecy surrounding some support groups, such as AA, also creates a kind of mystery around the meetings. Unless the husband attends the meetings with her, he doesn't really know what goes on there and whom his wife is cavorting with. If the meetings get extended, as they frequently do, when members go for coffee and further conversation afterward, a one-hour meeting turns into four hours away from home.

The recovering alcoholic makes a whole new set of friends with whom she has a strong and unique connection—one that the sober person will never fully comprehend. It's a club that no one really wants to be a member of, but, as with any club, if you are not in it, you will feel excluded. Alcoholics know what it's like to want a drink so much they can taste it, and although support groups such as AA caution against it, the bonds one makes with others in recovery can sometimes blossom into romantic relationships. This is why one husband of an alcoholic I knew wanted his wife to go to women-only meetings. Even if you aren't married, a good rule of thumb is not to date a member until you are at least two years sober, because if one of you falls off the wagon, you could take the other with you.

The best way to deal with jealousy or suspicion during your recovery is to invite your husband to go with you to an open meeting so that he can see what goes on there. Encourage your family to go to Al-Anon meetings as well so that they will understand the steps and the process for both the alcoholic and the people who love and care about her. If you are the parent of an alcoholic, go to Families Anonymous. (Alateen is for kids whose parents are alcoholics.) As part of the support network, your husband and family won't feel left out or neglected. Go to dinner as a couple with your sponsor or friends you've met at the meetings so that your spouse can form a bond with them. Whatever you do, don't shut your family out of the process. They have been witnesses to your problem or perhaps a part of it, so let them be part of the solution. Let them share in the abundance of gratitude, joy, and excitement that comes with your recovery.

My father used to go to recovery meetings with me because he found them inspirational. He told me after his first meeting that he felt that everyone should live by the twelve-step program, whether or not the person has an addiction problem. Making amends and reestablishing a spiritual connection can be good for anyone. Support groups or meetings should not be viewed as some kind of secret cult. Family members who share your experience firsthand are more likely to embrace this part of your new life with open arms.

At our campus recovery center, we have what is called a "Celebration of Recovery" every Thursday night. It's a meeting that is open to the community, students, family, and friends. It is almost always standing-room only. People come to hear about other people's recovery and find inspiration from other families' struggles and triumphs. Fortunately, nowadays people are much more open about being in recovery and are willing to proudly announce the years, days, or minutes since they've taken their last drink.

Al-Anon Members Speak Out

The following comments were posted on www.al-anonfamily-groups.org/. These candid and inspirational passages illustrate the fear, sadness, and feelings of powerlessness that many family members experience when trying to help their loved ones (and themselves) battle the compulsive cycle of alcoholism. Below is a list of what they think are the most important points on the road to recovery:

Admit your denial.

Read the Big Book, go to meetings, and don't drink.

Share your secrets.

Don't complicate the program.

Don't take yourself too seriously.

Spend as much time working your recovery program as you did drinking.

Choose a few motivational books to read each day that support your recovery and your desire to change.

Step One: We admitted we were powerless over alcohol and that our lives had become unmanageable. After all these years in Al-Anon, one would think that my life would now be manageable. Time and time again, however, I find myself wondering, "What am I to do next? Who do I need to fix now? Why does my life turn back to its unmanageable state?" Sometimes it is because I don't know what to do or not do regarding newly discovered alcoholism in a friend or family member. Sometimes it is because I become obsessed with helping a whole host of people— even though those people never asked for my help. Sometimes even service in Al-Anon gets so intense that I lose all sense of priority and importance.

At least now I am aware when I return to my unmanageable state. Being aware is the gift that Al-Anon has given me. Once aware, I pause. I stop what I am doing. Sometimes I just get out of the house for awhile. I take a walk or work in the garden. I give it a rest, so to speak. Sometimes I call an Al-Anon friend and vent my frustrations. Most recently, on discovering that a close relative's drinking problem was much more severe [than] I had thought[,] I just stopped thinking about the problem for several days. I sort of took a vacation from the problem. I discovered that what took years to break wasn't going to be fixed in a day, week, or perhaps year. I was able to pray about the situation. I was able to talk to a family member about the situation. At least now I am okay with myself. I know that I can accept the things that I cannot change.

—*Richard*

My marriage was falling apart. I was convinced my wife was the problem. My wife was convinced I was the problem. I never considered that both of us may be wrong. A friend referred me to an Al-Anon adult children's group. I was not living in active alcoholism; I had grown up in it. When I first heard Step One, which told me to replace the words "powerless over alcohol" with "powerless over people[,] places[,] and things," that made sense to me. But I was still not convinced I was powerless. I believed if I just did the right thing, I could favorably influence the people and circumstances in my life.

As time passed, I began seeing the more I did the worse things got. I found myself doing the same things again and again expecting different results. I was told this was insanity. I soon realized my fundamental problem was not just what I was doing, but my distorted thinking. It was my distorted thinking that led to my actions, and my actions were contributing to my problems by not resolving them.

When I tried to change my thinking, I was quickly convinced that I was powerless. Even when I was convinced my thinking was incorrect, I found it difficult to change. The thoughts had been ingrained into my very being. I was told to keep coming back. I did keep coming back, and over time as members in my group shared their experience, strength and hope, my thinking changed. As my thinking improved, my reactions and behaviors improved. Adversity and problems still occur in my life, but most of the time I no longer contribute to them.

—Chris

When I first came to Al-Anon, I felt like I had the weight of the world on my shoulders. I never lived my life for myself, but instead I was always there for others whenever they needed me, at any cost. I constantly lived in the pain that comes from watching my family struggle with this disease. I realized that although my intentions were good, I was fighting the wrong battles. It is futile to try to stop the progression of this disease in others and, when I try to do so, I sacrifice my own health and well being. I realized that being powerless over alcohol is admitting that the disease of alcoholism affects me as well as my family members. Because dealing with alcoholism means dealing with things like depression, low self-esteem and feelings of hopelessness, this disease is as progressive and potentially as fatal for me as it is for my family members. I realized that I need help learning to live my own life. Something had to change.

—Beverly

Alcoholics and addicts are not powerless. If that were true they would never get sober. They have the power to decide to stop using. Recovering individuals demonstrate the power of decision every day. The word "powerless" for addicts and alcoholics is a crutch and gives way to the "poor me syndrome."

"Powerless" when applied to the family and friends of addicts and alcoholics is absolutely on point. As a family member of an alcoholic or addict, one is "powerless" over the addiction and one's life can become unmanageable due to the chaos of addiction and the relationship and dynamics of addiction. It gives me great relief to finally acknowledge that I am powerless over the addict's behavior and decision to remain in active addiction.

I, however, possess the power to make the decision to change my behavior as it relates to my family member's addiction. It is a commitment to me to let go of a perceived responsibility, my involvement or effort to help the addict. An addict will only seek help when he/she is ready. The addict has the "power" to decide to do something different and it is that simple.

There is no magic wand or cure-all drug that will cause an addict to resist alcohol. It is merely the decision to stop. We can say things like stop the insanity, stop the chaos, or whatever one-liner we can think of, but it comes down to the simplicity of deciding to stop the cycle of addiction. It is just as simplistic for the family member to decide to stop the cycle too. It might be complicated and messy, but it can be done. Mentally separating oneself from the addict's behavior, severing yourself from the responsibility of your loved one's addiction by admitting your life has become unmanageable and you are powerless over your loved one's addiction is a first step.

—*Karen*

Today I attended my first Al-Anon meeting. I was scared and very emotional. I entered the door and it was a very real feeling that came over me, that "wow" I am really here ready to face a new step in making my life about me and changing what I can change and having the courage to admit that. For years I have always seen myself as the one who fixed everything and handled it all, now I am facing the fact that I cannot fix those with the addiction and that I now have to focus on me. It was a very overwhelming one hour in my life. I am going back next week and I know that each day it will get better. I think one of the most overwhelming feelings was finally realizing that I am truly not alone.

—*Angela*

I've always known I was powerless over alcohol. I learned that from my mother. I learned to be quiet and not complain. I learned to keep the family secrets. As I got older, I realized my life had become unmanageable. Even though I acted as though the disease didn't affect me—it had. I had never learned to take care of myself. I had learned to take care of others who suffered from this disease.

I didn't realize until years later that my mother was an "adult child" who had suffered much physical and emotional abuse as the result of alcohol. I lived with emotional abuse, and didn't understand what I had done wrong. Nothing I did was ever good enough. I've learned that, as a small child, I was powerless to change the feelings I was taught, and I've learned that as an adult, I have the ability to change those feelings. Through prayer and meditation, attending meetings, sharing with my sponsor, being of service to my district, and through the support of my service sponsor, I am finally learning to manage my feelings.

—*Kat*

Afterword

As I said in the beginning of this book, pain is an inevitable part of life. Even learning to walk requires falling down every once in a while. No one escapes it. But it's how you choose to deal with your pain that separates the sober from the alcoholic. If you are hurting now and are self-medicating with liquor, I hope you can find a way out of the darkness and into the path of recovery. I hope this book has inspired you to reach out for help, find healthy ways to cope with your pain, to improve your self-esteem, and to invest in your resiliency.

The road you take depends on the decision you make. Recovery forces us to throw away our crutches and face life on its terms, whatever they may be and no matter how formidable. It forces us out of our denial and into the reality of the mess we have often made of our lives and, all too often, the lives of those around us. It pushes us to the edge and begs us to see past the pain, the drinking, the desire to feel "normal," the negative consequences, and the agonizing shame.

I know all too well that recovery is not easy. But it is far easier than living as an alcoholic in fear, in isolation, and in desperation. My own struggle with fear and anxiety more than 32 years ago was so overwhelming that I chose to find relief in a wine bottle. For several years, alcohol provided me a way to cope with my fear, and the thought of being without it was like throwing away a life-raft while drowning. I was not sure I if I *wanted* to quit, or if I possessed the strength and willpower to do so. But I did. I made it that first day, and the second, and the last 11,500 and counting!

Consider how your life might be different without alcohol. When I went into rehab, there was a sign on the wall in one of the group rooms that said: "Alcohol gave me the wings to fly, and then it took away my sky." I would sit in the group every day and read that over and over again until I truly understood what it meant. Alcohol had given me the courage I lacked; an exaggerated sense of security that I mistook for ambition. For several years it worked; I was successful professionally and I began to climb the academic ladder. But then the wine took away my sky and I plummeted to the ground with nowhere to fly. It finally dawned on me that I could soar to great heights on my own. I realized if I could go a day, a month, and finally a year without the wine that had been my wings, then I could go the rest of my life. It was a humbling revelation and I thank God for giving me the strength.

I got my better self back and I know that you can find that better person inside you as well. As women we touch many more lives than just our own, whether it's a spouse, partner, children, grandchildren, friend, or community. Like a stone tossed in a pond, what we do creates a ripple effect on those around us. As mothers we have an obligation to our kids, who not only depend on us, but also look up to us as role models. Ask yourself, are you the kind of person who you want your children to be when they grow up? Are you teaching your children the right values and morals that they need in order to be healthy, functioning adults?

Recovery builds in us the resiliency necessary to bounce back when life knocks us down. Some days will be easy and others will rock your soul to its core, but the resiliency that comes with recovery will prepare you for those challenging days. There will be days when you are tempted to reach for that bottle instead of the phone to call your sponsor or a supportive friend. When this happens, get yourself to a twelve-step meeting, a support group or whoever and whatever you have enlisted as your safety net.

I encourage you to take the women's stories and advice in this book to heart and to let them help you take control of your life. It doesn't matter if you're a Girl Gone Wild, Barhopper, Momtini Mom, or a Closet Lush, make a decision today to move yourself out of that dark place. The road to recovery is open to anyone who is willing to travel on it. It is there for anyone who is willing to commit to a life that isn't numbed by alcohol and the resulting chaos that it causes you and everyone around you.

Go to the mirror right now and say out loud, "I do not have to live this way any longer!" Pick up the phone and call a friend or any of the resources that are in this book. Make the decision to live the life that you were created to live—a life without liquor. Choose to be healthy in both mind and body—to flourish and to be who you really are.

My sponsor used to tell me: "Kitty, you are responsible for the amount of light that you have seen." Now that you have read this book you are responsible for knowing that there is an answer, a solution, and a way out of the darkness. Do not be afraid; do not give in to that voice inside you that says that you cannot do this. Make that commitment, make that phone call, make that move to reclaim your life and your sky.

Getting Help: Resources for Recovery

General Resources for Alcoholics and Their Families

Whenever the question of getting professional help comes up, whether it's attending AA or going to some other support group, the resistant alcoholic will say, "I'd like to, but I don't have the time or the money." If you think you can't take a few weeks or months out of your drunken life to get sober, you're not ready. If you don't have money for a high-end residential rehab, there are organizations that will help you find the right facility or program for your budget.

Help for the alcoholic or the addict is everywhere nowadays, so no one should ever have to suffer alone or go untreated. Following is a selection of the best support groups and treatment centers for addiction in the country. If you or a loved one has a problem, do not wait one second longer to get help. Start by visiting the websites listed here to find a group or a facility that is a good fit for your individual issues. Then call for an appointment or simply to talk to someone who can guide you in the right direction, which is toward a lifetime of sobriety!

Support Groups

- AA World Services, Inc.
  www.aa.org
  (212) 870-3400
  P.O. Box 459
  New York, NY 10163

  If you go to the website, click the "Find a Meeting" button for a
  list of meetings, times, and locations in your area. If you call, ask
  them to mail you a list. Don't wait for the list to arrive by snail-
  mail, however; ask the person on the phone to locate a meeting
  near you, so that you can go immediately.

- National Institute on Alcohol Abuse and Alcoholism
  www.niaaa.nih.gov
  (301) 443-3860
  5635 Fishers Lane, MSC 9304
  Bethesda, MD 20892-9304

  *National Institute on Alcohol Abuse and Alcoholism: A Women's
  Health Issue Brochure*
  http://pubs.niaaa.nih.gov/publications/brochurewomen/women.
  htm

- Narcotics Anonymous World Services
  www.na.org
  (818) 773-9999
  P.O. Box 9999
  Van Nuys, CA 91409

- Al-Anon Family Group Headquarters, Inc. (also for Alateen)
  www.al-anon.org
  (888) 425-2666
  1600 Corporate Landing Parkway
  Virginia Beach, VA 23454-5617

- Cocaine Anonymous World Services
  www.ca.org
  (310) 559-5833
  21720 S. Wilmington Avenue, Suite 304
  Long Beach, CA 90810-1641

- Co-Dependents Anonymous Fellowship Services Office
  www.coda.org
  (888) 444-2359
  P.O. Box 33577
  Phoenix, AZ 85067-3577

- National Association for Children of Alcoholics
  www.nacoa.org
  888-55-4COAS
  10920 Connecticut Avenue, Suite 100
  Kensington, MD 20895

- Families Anonymous, Inc.
  www.familiesanonymous.org
  (800) 736-9805
  P.O. Box 3475
  Culver City, CA 90231-3475

- Overeaters Anonymous, Inc.
  www.oa.org
  505-891-2664
  P.O. Box 44020
  Rio Rancho, NM 87174-4020

Other Links

- Link to alcohol screening: http://pubs.niaaa.nih.gov/publications/aa65/AA65.pdf
- Link to drug abuse screening test: www.drtepp.com/pdf/substance_abuse.pdf
- The *Addiction Recovery Guide: Resources* includes evaluations, treatment options, sober living facilities, and more: www.addictionrecoveryguide.org
- Addiction and recovery information for individuals, families, and health professionals; resources include self-assessments, definitions, and introductions to twelve-step programs: www.addictionsandrecovery.org

Treatment Centers

- Austin Recovery
  Austin, TX
  (800) 373-2081; (512) 697-8600
  www.austinrecovery.org

- Betty Ford Center
  Rancho Mirage, CA
  (800) 434-7365; (760) 773-4100
  www.bettyfordcenter.org

- Hazelden
  Center City and Plymouth, MN, and Newberg, OR
  (800) 257-7810
  www.hazelden.org

- Marin Services for Women
  Greenbrae, CA
  (866) 924-2220; (415) 924-5995
  www.marinservicesforwomen.org

- Orchid Recovery Center for Women
  Palm Springs, FL
  (888) 672-4435; (561) 433-2336
  www.orchidrecoverycenter.com

- The Ranch at Dove Tree
  Collegiate Treatment Program
  Lubbock, TX
  Phone: (800) 218-6727; (806) 746-6777
  www.ranchatdovetree.com

- The Meadows
  Wickenburg, AZ
  (866) 807-3778
  www.themeadows.org

- Residence Twelve
  Kirkland, WA
  (800) 776-5944; (425) 823-8844
  www.residencexii.org

Other Support Groups

Harm reduction, Abstinence, and Moderation Support Harm Reduction, Abstinence, and Moderation Support (HAMS) is a free, peer-led support group for anyone who wants to modify his or her drinking or quit altogether. There are seventeen elements to the HAMS program, which you can learn more about by going to its website. HAMS offers information and support through chat rooms and e-mail groups, as well as live meetings. The group also posts articles and videos on its website. Unlike AA, for which quitting as the ultimate goal, HAMS supports every positive change, no matter how minor, including safe drinking or reduced drinking.

The idea of harm reduction is based on a set of practical strategies intended to reduce the negative consequences of high-risk behaviors that come from drinking too much. Harm Reduction takes a nonjudgmental approach to addiction that works with whatever stage of drinking or drug use people are in at the moment. As the group says on its website: "Harm reduction accepts that high risk behaviors such as recreational alcohol intoxication are part of our world and works to minimize their harmful effects rather than simply ignore or condemn them. Harm reduction does not attempt to force people to change in ways which they do not choose for themselves. In other word, instead of one step at a time, HAMS believes in one baby step at a time. HAMS addresses the needs of people who are either unwilling or unable to abstain from alcohol. Similar to the stance against abstinence-only sex paradigms, Harm Reduction takes a more pragmatic approach to how people behave in our culture. For more information, visit www.hamsnetwork.org/ or call (347) 678-5671.

LifeRing Secular Recovery

LifeRing is a secular, international nonprofit organization that provides peer-run addiction recovery groups for anyone who wants to recover from alcohol and those who have a relationship with an addict or an alcoholic. LifeRing takes an experimental approach to maintaining abstinence, and its members are free to incorporate ideas from other recovery groups. It encourages members to use relapses as learning experiences and discourages admonishing members for relapsing. The LifeRing philosophy is based on three principles: sobriety, secularism, and self-help. Meetings do not open with prayers, and members do not have to believe in God or a Supreme Being. The principle of self-help involves developing an individual program of recovery. Unlike AA's twelve steps, members do not have sponsors, but there are meetings that you can go to, which are run by peers.

LifeRing uses the book *How Was Your Week*, which replaced the *Secular Handbook*. Family members and friends can join LifeRing Partners but are also welcome to attend meetings, provided they are clean and sober at the time of the meeting. For more information, visit lifering.org.

Moderation Management

According to its website, Moderation Management (MM) is a behavioral change program and a national support group network for people concerned about their drinking and who desire to make positive lifestyle changes. MM believes behaviors can be changed, and that alcohol abuse, versus dependence, is a learned behavior (habit) for problem drinkers and not a disease. MM empowers individuals to accept personal responsibility for choosing and maintaining their own paths, whether moderation or abstinence. MM promotes early recognition of risky drinking behavior and believes that moderate drinking is a more easily achievable goal.

Moderation Management, advocates say, is less costly, shorter in duration, less intensive, and has a higher success rate than the traditional abstinence-only approach. They believe that most people do not want to be labeled "alcoholics" and have real concerns about how their participation in twelve-step programs will affect their jobs and ability to attain future medical and life insurance. MM is seen as a less threatening first step and one that problem drinkers are more likely to attempt before their problems become overwhelming.

Approximately 30 percent of MM members go on to abstinence-based programs based on the disease model of alcohol dependence and "its reliance on the concept of powerlessness." MM members believe that these programs are particularly counterproductive for women and minorities, who often already feel like victims and powerless. They say studies show that professional programs that offer both moderation and abstinence have higher success rates than do those that are abstinence only.

This supportive mutual-help environment includes a nine-step professionally reviewed program, which provides information about alcohol, moderate drinking guidelines and limits, drink-monitoring exercises, goal-setting techniques, and self-management strategies. MM meetings are free of charge, but donations made by individual members and MM groups are used to support community and national programs. For more information, go to www.moderation.org.

Rational Recovery

Rational Recovery (RR) is an exclusive worldwide source of information, counseling, guidance, and direct instruction on independent recovery through planned, permanent abstinence. RR consists of a body of information about the nature of addiction and recovery, about the risk/benefit ratios of addiction treatment and recovery group participation, and about the social and political dynamics behind mainstream thinking about substance abuse and addiction recovery. It offers Addictive Voice Recognition Technique (AVRT), which is one of the guiding principles of Rational Recovery.

Unlike other support groups that depend in part on regular meetings, there are no Rational Recovery groups, RR treatment centers, or rehabs. In AVRT-based recovery, the alcoholic or the addict is on her own. RR advocates believe strongly that people's desire to attend recovery groups is based on the assumption that they will relapse if they do not attend meetings. AVRT-based recovery sees this form of "self-doubt" as an example of someone's

Addictive Voice. If you meet with others who have self-doubt and Addictive Voices, then you are only reinforcing that crippling, dependent belief.

Rational Recovery proponents are strongly opposed to addiction treatments because they believe that these are ineffective and can even do more harm than good. AVRT is also incompatible with other addiction treatments because it does not require that the alcoholic be diagnosed with a medical or psychological disease and provided with services aimed at reducing the desire to get high. Rational Recovery proponents do not train or certify counselors to teach RR or AVRT. Likewise, they are firmly opposed to interventions, wherein families "conspire, often under professional guidance, to force their addicted loved ones into worthless, expensive addiction-treatment programs. These unethical, melodramatic confrontations not only aggravate addiction and destroy bridges of reconciliation, but rarely produce secure abstinence."

Instead, Rational Recovery proponents encourage the zero-tolerance ultimatum, coupled with the firm expectation of immediate AVRT-based recovery. In this approach, the family simply confronts the addicted member with a choice between addiction and family membership. Although this may seem excessive or even cruel, the zero-tolerance ultimatum presumes that the addicted one is capable of moral conduct and loyalty to the family. Those interested in learning about the principles of RR and AVRT should go to the website, where they can take a course in its theories and applications (www.Rational.org; 530-621-2667 or 530-621-4374).

Secular Organizations for Sobriety

Secular Organizations for Sobriety (SOS) is a nonprofit network of autonomous, nonprofessional local groups dedicated solely to helping individuals achieve and maintain sobriety. There are group meetings in many cities throughout the country. SOS believes there should be a separation of church and state when it comes to sobriety and considers itself an alternative recovery program for alcoholics or drug addicts who are uncomfortable with the spiritual aspects of the twelve steps.

SOS credits the individual for achieving and maintaining his or her own sobriety and does not feel the necessity of giving props to a higher power, although it supports other recovery programs such as AA that are spiritually based. SOS encourages healthy skepticism and the use of the scientific methods to understand alcoholism. All of those who sincerely seek sobriety are welcome as members in any SOS Group. SOS seeks only to promote sobriety among people who suffer from alcoholism or other drug addictions.

Like RR, SOS considers sobriety an individual responsibility, but it does believe that the support of other alcoholics and addicts is a vital adjunct to recovery. In SOS, members share experiences, insights, information, strength, and encouragement in friendly, honest, anonymous, and supportive group meetings. To avoid unnecessary entanglements, each SOS group is self-supporting through contributions from its members and refuses outside support.

Its website provides more information about the organization, including the history and brochures about the group, as well as links to live meetings around the world. Visit www.cfiwest.org/sos/index.htm.

SMART Recovery

SMART Recovery, which stands for Self-Management and Recovery Training, helps people with all types of addictive behaviors, including alcoholism, drug abuse, substance abuse, gambling problems, and addictions to other substances and activities. It is a science- and research-based program that emphasizes the motivation to abstain, coping with urges, problem solving, and maintaining a balanced lifestyle. SMART does not view addiction as a disease and does not believe in using labels such as "alcoholic" or "addict." It stresses self-responsibility, self-motivation, and self-discipline as the primary means of stopping substance use. SMART Recovery offers free face-to-face mutual self-help groups and online help. The website provides more information about the group, as well as links to message boards, more than twenty online meetings, and more than six hundred face-to-face meetings around the world. Go to www.smartrecovery.org for more information.

Women For Sobriety

Women For Sobriety (WFS) was the first national self-help program for women alcoholics, and the organization now provides help for those with drug addictions. The WFS New Life program grew out of one woman's search for sobriety. Now, hundreds of WFS self-help groups are offered across this country and abroad. WFS is based on a thirteen-statement "Program of Positivity" that encourages emotional and spiritual growth; the New Life program has been effective in helping women overcome their alcoholism and adopt a new lifestyle. The program can also be used with hospitals, clinics, treatment facilities, women centers, or wherever alcoholics are being treated.

The idea of a women's-only recovery program evolved from the fact that the success rates for male alcoholics were higher than for females, leading to the mistaken conclusion that women were harder to treat and were less cooperative than male alcoholics. It became clear that women alcoholics need a different kind of recovery program than those being offered to men, and the success of the New Life program has shown that to be the case.

For additional information, including the New Life program and complete recovery catalog, please call 215-536-8026 or visit www.womenforsobriety.org.

Sixteen Steps for Discovery and Empowerment Model

Created by Charlotte Kasl, Ph.D., the sixteen steps for discovery and empowerment model is a holistic approach to overcoming addiction that encompasses a person's mind, body, and spirit.

Kasl's first book, *Women, Sex and Addiction: A Search for Love and Power*, has become a classic in the addiction field and has been a powerful source of hope and healing for thousands of women. Her book *Many Roads, One Journey: Moving beyond the Twelve Steps* revealed her sixteen-step empowerment approach for overcoming addiction and trauma. Her approach has many parallels to positive psychology, attachment theory, developing resilience, and respecting individual and cultural differences.

She states that "while fear may jump-start people into recovery, love and self respect are what helps them heal." The sixteen-step model helps people develop ego strength, which is seen as their having the ability to be introspective and to ask themselves such questions as: "Who am I?" "What do I value, believe, and want?" This method is based on the belief that a major task in recovering from addiction is to validate the underlying, positive survival goals for safety, connection, pleasure, love, and power that the addictive behavior used to accomplish and then to find nonaddictive and positive ways to meet those needs. The steps demonstrate how to take charge of your life and rebuild your self-esteem and self-worth. Please visit www.addictioninfo.org to learn more.

Alcoholism Literature

Healing and Hope: Six Women from the Betty Ford Center Share Their Powerful Journeys of Addiction and Recovery, by Betty Ford (Berkley).

Drinking: A Love Story, by Caroline Knapp (Dell).

Alcoholism, by Maria Gifford (Greenwood).

Happy Hours: Alcohol in a Woman's Life, by Devon Jersild (HarperCollins).

Emotional Sobriety: From Relationship Trauma to Resilience and Balance, by Tian Dayton (Health Communications).

Awakening Your Sexuality: A Guide for Recovering Women, by Stephanie S. Covington (Hazelden).

Addiction and Spirituality: A Multidisciplinary Approach, edited by Oliver J. Morgan and Merle R. Jordan (Chalice Press).

The Handbook of Addiction Treatment for Women, eds. Shulamith Lala Ashenberg Straussner and Stephanie Brown (Jossey-Bass).

Women in Alcoholics Anonymous: Recovery and Empowerment, by Jolen M.

Sanders (First Forum Press).

Getting Sober: A Practical Guide to Making It through the First 30 Days, by Kelly Madigan Erlandson (McGraw-Hill).

A Meditation to Support Your Recovery from Alcohol and Other Drugs, by Belleruth Naparstek (Health Journeys/CD).

Meditation for Busy People: Sixty Seconds to Serenity, by Dawn Groves (New World).

A Gradual Awakening, by Stephen Levine (Anchor).

Codependent No More: How to Stop Controlling Others and Start Caring for Yourself, by Melody Beattie (Hazelden).

Women, Sex and Addiction: A Search for Love and Power, by Charlotte Kasl (Harper Paperback).

Many Roads, One Journey: Moving beyond the Twelve Steps, by Charlotte Kasl (Harper Paperback).

Bibliography

Introduction

National Institutes of Health. *Alcohol: A Women's Health Issue* (DHHS Publication No. 03-4956). Washington, DC: U.S. Government Printing Office, 2008. Retrieved September 17, 2011. http://pubs.niaaa.nih.gov/publications/brochurewomen/women.htm#drinking.

Tsai, J., R. Floyd, P. Green, and C. Boyle. "Patterns and Average Volume of Alcohol Use Among Women of Childbearing Age." *Maternal & Child Health Journal*, 11(5), 437–445, 2007.

1. My Story

Alcoholics Anonymous World Services Inc. *Alcoholics Anonymous: The Story of How Many Thousands of Men and Women Have Recovered from Alcoholism*, 4th ed. New York: World Service Headquarters, 2001.

Fisher, C. *Wishful Drinking.* New York: Simon & Schuster, 2008.

Hanson, D. J. Alcohol: Problems and Solutions. "Bar Exam." Retrieved September 17, 2011. http://alcohol.bitglyph.com/BarExam.php.

Knapp, C. *Caroline's Drinking: A Love Story.* New York: Dell, 1996.

The Lost Weekend. Motion picture. Directed by B. Wilder. Paramount/Universal, Los Angeles, 1945.

The Paper Chase. Motion picture. Directed by G. Jenkins. 20th Century Fox, Los Angeles, 1973.

Zailckas, D. *Smashed: The Story of a Drunken Girlhood.* New York: Penguin Group, 2005.

2. Where Does It Hurt?

American Federation of Labor–Congress of Industrial Organizations. *Fact Sheet 2010.* "Professional Women: Vital Statistics." Retrieved September 17, 2011. www.pay-equity.org/PDFs/ProfWomen.pdf.

"Freedom from Bondage." Alcoholics Anonymous Big Book. www.aa.org.

Mayo Foundation for Medical Education and Research. "Depression in Women: Understanding the Gender Gap." Retrieved September 17, 2011. www.mayoclinic.com/health/depression/MH00035.

Mental Health America. "Depression in Women." Retrieved September 17, 2011. www.nmha.org/index.cfm?objectId=C7DF8CA2–1372–4D20-C8554FEA09A9FDEC.

National Institutes of Health. *Alcohol: A Women's Health Issue.*

Stop Bullying Now. "Learn What You Can Do." www.stopbullyingnow.com.

5. Binge Drinking

AlcoholPolicyMD.com. "American Medical Association Poll Finds Parents Outraged by Spring Break Promotions" (press release). www.alcoholpolicymd.com/press_room/Press_releases/pr_nr_3_07_02.htm.

Feliz, J. "More Than One in Five Parents Feel Ill-Equipped to Prevent Kids from Trying Drugs and Alcohol." September 14, 2010. Partnership at Drugfree.org. www.drugfree.org/newsroom/more-than-one-in-five-parents-feel-ill-equipped-to-prevent-kids-from-trying-drugs-and-alcohol.

Gostin, N. "Melissa Gilbert Shares Her Struggle to Get Sober as Drugfree.org Spokesperson." October 14, 2010. ParentDish. www.parentdish.com/2010/10/14/melissa-gilbert.

MetLife Foundation Attitude Tracking Study. "National Study Shows Increase in Teen Alcohol and Drug Abuse after a Decade Long Decline." March 2, 2010. www.prevention.org/Professionals/News/Default.asp.

Reitman, I., M. Simmons, and J. Landis. *Animal House.* Motion picture. Directed by J. Landis. Universal, Los Angeles, 1973.

Teen Drug Abuse. "The Health Effects of Teen Drug Abuse." www.teendrugabuse.us/teensandalcohol.html.

6. Mothers Who Drink

Addiction Intervention. "More Women Driving Drunk—Numbers Go Up 30 Percent." www.addiction-intervention.com/current-events/addiction-news/more-women-driving-drunk-numbers-up-30-percent.

Griffioen, J. D. "Happy Hour Play Dates" in the New York Times: Is Drinking Around Your Kids a Sign of Problems?" November 9, 2006. ParentDish. www.parentdish.com/2006/11/09/happy-hour-playgroups-in-the-new-york-times.

Mellor, C. *The Three-Martini Playdate: A Practical Guide to Parenting.* San Francisco: Chronicle Books, 2004.

Mommy Wants Vodka (blog), www.mommywantsvodka.com.

Mothers for Social Drinking. Mission statement. www.muchmorethanamom.com/2007/02/04/mothers-for-social-drinking.

Senior, J. "All Joy and No Fun: Why Parents Hate Parenting." *New York*, July 4, 2010. http://nymag.com/print/?/news/features/67024.

Wilder-Taylor, S. *Naptime Is the New Happy Hour: And Other Ways Toddlers Turn Your Life Upside Down.* New York: Simon and Schuster, 2008.

7. Drunkorexia

"Drunkorexia." *Lainey Gossip: Calling All Smuthounds* (blog). July 3, 2006. www.laineygossip.com.

Freedman, R., and K. Barnouin. *Skinny Bitch.* Philadelphia: Running Books, 2005.

The Fresh Story (blog). "Drunkorexia." February 3, 2009. http://freshstory.org/blogs/freshstory.php?p=35&more=1&c=1&tb=1&pb=1.

Jennings, A. "Drunkorexia: Alcohol Mixes with Eating Disorders." October 21, 2010. ABC News.com. http://abcnews.go.com/Health/drunkorexia-alcohol-mixes-eating-disorders/story?id=11936398.

Krenshaw, S. "Starving Themselves, Cocktail in Hand." *New York Times.* March, 3, 2002. www.nytimes.com/2008/03/02/fashion/02drunk.html.

Wang, L., I. M. Lee, J. E. Manson, J. E. Buring, and H. D. Sesso. "Alcohol Consumption, Weight Gain, and Risk of Becoming Overweight in Middle-Aged and Older Women." *Archives of Internal Medicine, 170* (5) 453–461, 2010. doi:10.1001/archinternmed.2009.527.

8. When Bad Things Happen to Drunk Women

Emanuele, M., F. Wezeman, and N. V. Emanuele. "Alcohol's Effects on Female Reproductive Function." *Alcohol Research and Health, 26*(4), 274–281, 2002.

Hingson, R. W., T. Heeren, R. C. Zakocs, A. Kopstein, and H. Wechsler. "Magnitude of Alcohol-Related Mortality and Morbidity Among

U.S. College Students Ages 18–24." *Journal of Studies on Alcohol,* 63(2), 136–144, 2002.

Kwan, M. L., L. H. Kushi, and E. Weltzien et al. "Alcohol Consumption and Breast Cancer Recurrence and Survival Among Women with Early-Stage Breast Cancer: The Life After Cancer Epidemiology Study." *Journal of Oncology,* 28(29), 4410–4416, 2010. doi: 10.1200/ JCO.2010.29.2730.

National Association of Treatment Providers. "Treatment Is the Answer: A White Paper on the Cost-Effectiveness of Alcoholism and Drug Dependency." Laguna Hills, CA, 1991.

National Institutes of Health. *Alcohol: A Women's Health Issue.*

Tsai, V. W., C. L. Anderson, and F. E. Vaca. "Alcohol Involvement Among Young Female Drivers in US Fatal Crashes: Unfavorable Trends." *Injury Prevention, 16,* 17–20, 2010. doi: 10.1136/ip.2009.022301.

Baabor, T. F., J. C. Higgins-Biddle, J. B. Saunders, and M. G. Monteiro. "The Alcohol Use Disorders Identification Test (AUDIT): Guidelines for Use in Primary Care." World Health Organization, Department of Mental Health and Substance Dependence. http://whqlibdoc.who. int/hq/2001/who_msd_msb_01.6a.pdf.

Ewing, J. "Detecting Alcoholism. The CAGE Questionnaire." *Journal of the American Medical Association, 252*(14), 1905–1907, 1984.

National Institutes of Alcohol Abuse and Alcoholism. "Alcohol Alert." No. 65, April 2005. http://pubs.niaaa.nih.gov/publications/aa65/ AA65.htm.

Saunders, J. B., O. G. Aasland, T. F. Babor, and J. R. de la Fuente. "Development of the Alcohol Use Disorders Identification Test (AUDIT): WHO Collaborative Project on Early Detection of Persons with Harmful Alcohol Consumption: II. *Addiction, 88*(6), 791–804, 1993. doi:10.1111/j.1360–0443.1993.tb02093.x.

10. Recovery Strategies

Benson, H. *The Relaxation Response.* New York: HarperCollins, 2001.

Headey, B., R. Muffels, and G. G. Wagner. "Long-running German Panel Survey Shows That Personal and Economic Choices, Not Just Genes, Matter for Happiness." *Proceedings of the National Academy of Sciences of the United States of America, 107*(42),17922–17962, October 2010. doi:10.1073/pnas.1008612107.

Ornish, D. *The Spectrum: A Scientifically Proven Program to Feel Better, Live Longer, Lose Weight, and Gain Health.* New York: Random House, 2007.

Weil, Andrew. *Eight Weeks to Optimum Health: A Proven Program for Taking Full Advantage of You Body's Natural Healing Power.* New York: Random House, 2006.

11. Staying Sober: Alcoholics Anonymous and Other Programs

Laudet, A. B. "The Impact of Alcoholics Anonymous on Other Substance abuse Related Twelve-Step Programs." *Recent Developments in Alcoholism, 18* 71–89, 2008.

Marshall, Shelly. Day by Day. www.day-by-day.org/index.html.

Twelve Steps and Twelve Traditions. New York: Alcoholics Anonymous World Services, 1952.

Index